access English 1

Jill Baker · Clare Constant · David Kitchen

Investigating Words section: Louise Dempsey · Isabel Wright

Heinemann

Contents

Part C: Investigating Words

The following icons are used in this book

 This activity is supported by the Investigating Words section

 There are worksheets to support this activity

1 Shaping stories

1.1

This unit will help you to:
- tell someone a story
- see how stories are shaped
- shape and write a story

Telling stories

This section will help you to:
- explore the five main things you must say when you tell a story
- tell someone a story about something that happened to you
- write a question using a capital letter and a question mark

1 **Work as a class. Share your answers to these questions.**

> **1** What stories have you already told today? *Maybe you told someone about something that happened to you.*
>
> **2** What stories have you heard today? *Perhaps a friend told you about a film on TV.*

2 **Work as a class. Read this story a student told. Then answer the question.**

> **1** Read the notes around the story. Talk about how the story-teller gave you the information.
>
> **2** What *five* things must you say when you tell a story?

Night fright

1 When it happened.

2 Where it happened.

Last night I was asleep and I woke up suddenly ... and I was sure there was someone trying to get into my bedroom ... I could see this black thing coming through the curtain and I was really scared
5 ... I couldn't do anything ... I couldn't even yell ... then the black thing jumped on my bed – it was the cat.

3 Who it is about.

4 What happened.

5 Why it made you feel this way.

WS 3
1.1

Work in pairs. You are going to tell the story of this cartoon. Look at it carefully, then do the work below.

1 Make up answers to these questions.
   a **When** did this story happen? *Last night? Last week?...*
   b **Who** is in this story? *A boy in my class called...*
   c **Where** did this story happen?
   d **What** happened? *Asif was supposed to ... but ...*
   e **Why** did this make the dad so angry?

2 Tell your story to another pair. Use your answers to help you.

WS 4
1.1

Work in pairs. You are going to tell a story to your partner.

1 Choose one of these ideas for your story:
   • a time when you felt very happy
   • a time when you felt very angry
   • a time when you felt really embarrassed
   • a time when you felt really scared.

> **Remember**
> • A question must begin with a capital letter.
> • A question must end with a question mark.
>   *Who is the story about?*

2 Write *five* questions that will help you plan what to say:
   • When ...? • Who ...? • Where ...? • What ...? • Why ...?

p. 179

3 Work out the answers to your five questions. Tell your story to your partner.

5 **Work as a class. What *five* things should you remember to say when you tell a story?**

How writers shape stories

This section will help you to:
- look at the different stages in a written story
- understand how a writer builds up to the story's ending

1 Work as a class. Brainstorm all the things writers should do when they write stories.

- *Use characters …*   • *Use sentences …*   • *…*

2 Work as a class. Many stories are made up of five stages. Read this chart. Then read the explanation box and do the work opposite.

Story stages	Example: Cinderella
1 Opening The scene is set: *Who? When? Where?*	Cinderella, once upon a time, at her father's house.
2 Development Something happens that causes a problem: *What?* *Why is this a problem?*	Prince Charming's party invitation arrives. Cinderella has no dress and is not allowed to go.
3 Someone tries to sort out the problem: *Who?* *How?*	Cinderella's fairy godmother makes her a magic dress so she can go to the party. The magic will end at midnight.
4 But things get even worse: *How?*	Prince Charming falls in love with Cinderella. She forgets she must leave before the clock strikes twelve. At midnight she runs off, dropping her shoe. He finds the shoe but he doesn't know who she is.
5 Conclusion Things get sorted out – happily or unhappily: *How are they sorted out?*	The Prince searches for the only woman the shoe will fit. He finds Cinderella.

1 Read the Explanation box above.

2 Listen to your teacher read *Boo!*. What happens in each of its five stages? What would you write in a chart like the one opposite?

3 What does the reader only find out right at the end? Is this a good way to end the story?

Boo!

She didn't like it at all when her father had to go down to London and, for the first time, she had to sleep alone in the old house.

She went up to her bedroom early. She turned the key
5 and locked the door. She **latched** the windows and drew the curtains. She peered inside her wardrobe, and pulled open the bottom drawer of her chest-of-drawers; she got down on her knees and looked under the bed.

She undressed; she put on her nightdress.

10 She pulled back the heavy **linen** cover and climbed into bed. Not to read but to try and sleep – she wanted to sleep as soon as she could. She reached out and turned off the lamp.

'That's good,' said a little voice. 'Now we're safely locked
15 in for the night.'

Stage 1 The scene is set: **Who? When? Where?**

Stage 2 Something happens that causes a problem: **What? Why** is this a problem?

Stage 3 Someone tries to sort out the problem: **Who? How?**

Stage 4 But things get even worse: **How?**

Stage 5 Things get sorted out – happily or unhappily: **How?**

Taken from *Short!* by Kevin Crossley-Holland

latched – locked
linen – a type of cloth

Work in pairs. Listen to the story. At the end of each part your teacher will stop.

> **1** Work out which stage of the story you have just heard.
>
> **2** Copy out and complete the sentences.

In the back seat

Part 1

Abby's my best friend and this happened to her sister, and Abby told me about it, so I know it's true.

Her sister's eighteen and she's got a car, and she's called Rachel. Last week, well, she went to a late night party. Somewhere in town, I don't know where
5 exactly, and it ended very late. About two o'clock.

1 This is the _____. It tells you the story is about (*who?*) _____
(*when?*) _____ (*where?*) _____.

Part 2

By the time Rachel drove home, the city was all empty. That's spooky! Anyhow, Rachel got going and she looked in her mirror, and there was this truck kind-of-thing, right behind her. She could see the driver, and he was big and leaning forward and well ... he started flashing her: headlights,
10 dipped lights, no lights. No lights in the dark, that's really dangerous. Well, the man kept flashing her and Rachel didn't know what to do.

2 What happens is _____. This causes a problem because _____.

Part 3

She just drove as fast as she could. But when she turned left, the man turned left. Then Rachel turned into Lake Street, that's where Abby lives, and this man turned right as well. He even followed her into her
15 own driveway.

Rachel just put her hand on the horn and never took it off. In the middle of the night. Her dad woke straight up and he came rushing down to find out what was going on.

'That man!' cried Rachel. 'He's been following me and flashing me right
20 across town.'

3 _____ tries to sort out the problem by _____ and by
_____.

Part 4

Then the driver got out of his truck kind-of-thing. He was big and he had a scar on one cheek – you could see the stitches. 'Quick!' he said. 'There's a man in her back seat, I flashed her every time I saw him raise the axe.'

4 Things get even worse because _____.

Part 5

25 Then Abby's father yelled and just dragged Rachel out of the car. And the driver with the scar, he ripped open the back door and fell on the man hiding there.

5 This is the ending. Things are sorted out happily when _____. This ending works well because _____.

Taken from *Short!* by Kevin Crossley-Holland

4 **Work in pairs. Can you remember what the five stages of a story are? Explain them to your partner.**

Planning a story

This section will help you to:
- plan a five-stage story
- work out an ending that will surprise readers
- discuss how writing and telling a story are different

1 Work as a class. What do you already know? Talk about these questions.

1 What is the difference between writing a story and telling a story?

2 What are the *five* stages of many written stories?

2 Work as a class. You can plan a story using the five stages to help you. Read the example below. Then answer the question.

1 How else could the story end? Think of another ending. You may wish to change the information you hide until the end.

Story stages	Plan
1 Opening The scene is set: *Who is the story about?* *When does it take place?* *Where does it take place?*	Kelly, aged twelve, her brother Dan, Mum, and their dog Fizzy. Just before Dan's ninth birthday. Kelly is in the lounge with Fizzy.
2 Development Something happens that causes a problem: *What? Why is this is a problem?*	Mum comes home with Dan's birthday present. It is a Game Boy Advanced. Mum must hide it from Dan.
3 Someone tries to sort out the problem. *Who? How?*	Kelly has an idea. She hides it under the sofa.
4 But things get even worse: *How?*	But on Dan's birthday Kelly can't find the present. Mum is very cross.
5 Conclusion Things get sorted out – happily or unhappily: *How?*	Unhappily Kelly finds Fizzy sitting in her basket chewing the Game Boy Advanced like a bone.
What piece(s) of important information will you hide until the end?	Fizzy had taken the Game Boy Advanced out from under the sofa.

WS 3
1.3

Work in pairs. Put these pictures in the right order to tell a story.

WS 4
1.2

Now work on your own. Write a plan of the story you have just worked out. Write your plan in a chart like the one opposite.

Story stages	Plan
1 Opening The scene is set: *Who? When? Where?*	*Karen, 20 years old …*

5

Work as a class. Talk about what you need to do when you plan a story.

1.4 Writing a story

This section will help you to:
- start to write a story
- write in sentences
- use full stops and capital letters to show where one sentence ends and another begins
- use the past tense

1 Work as a class. You are going to write the story you have planned.

> **1** You should write in the past tense. Brainstorm a list of verbs that are in the past tense, for example: *walked, rode, had said …*
>
> **2** You should write in sentences. What do you know about writing in sentences? For example: *You begin with …*

2 Work as a class. Read this flow chart. Find out how to make sure you write in sentences for your story. Then do the work below.

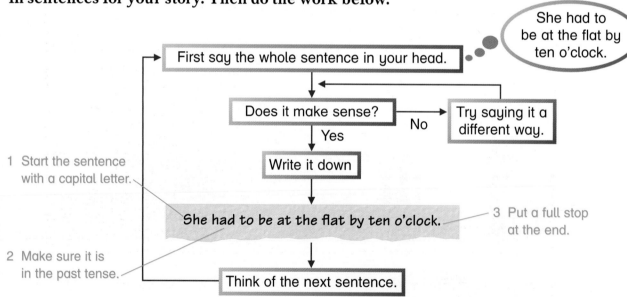

She had to be at the flat by ten o'clock.

First say the whole sentence in your head.

Does it make sense? — No → Try saying it a different way.

Yes

Write it down

1 Start the sentence with a capital letter.

2 Make sure it is in the past tense.

She had to be at the flat by ten o'clock.

3 Put a full stop at the end.

Think of the next sentence.

1 What do you have to do to write a sentence?

2 Write three more sentences for the opening of the story, describing this scene.

Where?

Who?

When?

WS 3
1.4

Work in pairs. Take it in turns to write the *four* missing sentences about Karen.

> 1 Say your sentence out loud.
>
> 2 Check with your partner that it makes sense.
>
> 3 Check that it is in the past tense.
>
> 4 Write the whole sentence down.
>
> Karen wanted to find somewhere to live. It had _____. She had looked in the newspaper for somewhere to rent. _____. She could not afford much. _____. She had phoned up the landlord. _____.

WS 4
1.4

Now work on your own. Write *five* sentences to tell this next part of the story. Make sure you keep to the past tense: *Karen decided to rent it.*

5

Work in pairs. Read and check your partner's five sentences.

> 1 Tick the sentences that make sense.
>
> 2 Circle every capital letter that begins a sentence.
>
> 3 Circle every full stop that ends a sentence.
>
> 4 Put in any missing capital letters or full stops.
>
> 5 Underline any verbs that are not in the past tense.

Writing in paragraphs

This section will help you to:
- complete your story
- work out when to write a new paragraph
- know how to set out a new paragraph

1 Work as a class. Talk about what you already know about writing in paragraphs.

2 Work as a class. First read the explanation box. Then read the next part of the story. Explain why the writer needed to start each new paragraph.

> **Explanation**
> Start a new paragraph when you write about a different:
> - place
> - time
> - person
> - idea
>
> or when you start a new speech.

Flat hunt

It was very early in the morning. Karen had to be at the flat by ten o'clock and she did not know the way. She saw the sign for Leeds Town Centre and came off the motorway.

5 **Half an hour later** Karen spotted 47 Wilting Gardens. It was in a rough part of town. That was why the flat was so cheap to rent.

Mark Kreep was waiting outside when she got there. He smiled and said hello.

10 'Hello,' said Karen.

1 These sentences are all about Karen driving to the flat.

2 Stop! Leave a line before you write about a new place, person, time or idea.

3 Begin with a sentence which shows why it is a new paragraph.

4 When someone starts speaking, begin a new line.

Work in pairs. Read the text below. Then answer the questions below.

1 Where should this writer have started a new paragraph?
Find *at least six* places.

2 Explain why a new paragraph is needed each time.

> New paragraph needed because writing about a different place.

Remember
Start a new paragraph when you write about a new place, person, time or idea.

Karen did not like the look of Mark Kreep very much. He had greasy hair and a strange smile. If she took the flat she hoped she would not have to see him very often. Mark showed her round the flat. It had everything
5 Karen wanted but it was very dirty. When they were outside again she said, 'It's okay but it needs cleaning.' Mark looked at her and said, 'I would get it cleaned before you move in.' Karen thought carefully. The rent was okay. She could make the flat look nice. 'I'll take it,'
10 she said. Later she told her dad about the flat. He was very worried. 'That's a very rough part of town. Will you be safe?' he asked. That got Karen thinking.

4

**Now work on your own.
Write the end of the story
about these two pictures.**

5 **Work as a class. Talk about what you have learned.**

1 How do you know when to start a new paragraph?

2 How do you show a new paragraph?

3 Look at the end of your story. Where did you begin a new paragraph?
Why? Explain it to the rest of the class.

2

Active reading

This unit will help you to:
- picture the situation in a story
- predict (guess) what might happen
- read between the lines

2.1 Finding evidence in the text

This section will help you to:
- make sense of what you read
- picture in your mind a situation from a story
- work out what you definitely know about a story

1 Work as a class. What is your favourite story? Talk about how it starts.

2 Work as a class. It is important to get a picture of what is happening in a story. Read the paragraph opposite. It is the first paragraph of a novel. Then do the work below.

   1 Choose *one* thing that you definitely know from this opening.
   2 Look at the picture.
      • Find *one* thing that the artist has got right.
      • Find *one* thing that the artist has left out.

3 Work in pairs.

   1 What other things can you definitely know from the opening?
   2 What else has the artist got wrong in the picture?

4 Work on your own. List the things you have found out. Use these headings.

- Name of boy in story:
- Who he is with:
- Where they are:
- Time of year:
- Weather:
- Where they are going:

Joshua on the move

The last place Joshua Parker wanted to be on a sunny day in late July was sitting in a car, stuck in heavy traffic, heading north on the M1. Cars towing trailers and caravans clogged the lane in front, almost bringing it to a standstill. Holiday traffic. But Josh was not going on holiday. He was being driven away from his friends, his summer, kidnapped by his own mother.

Taken from *Truth or Dare* by Celia Rees

5   **Work as a class. Share the information you have collected.**
Are you sure about what you definitely know?

Predict what might happen

This section will help you to:
- read between the lines
- predict what might be happening
- use writing to explore ideas

1 Work as a class. Writers give you information at the start of a story. List the things you knew for sure about the start of the story on page 17.

2 Work as a class. A writer may also want to get you guessing. Read about Josh and his mother again, below. Then talk about what you think might be happening as you read between the lines.

1 How might you feel if you were Josh?
2 What might be going to happen?

1 To where?
Family? New job for mum?

The last place Joshua Parker wanted to be on a sunny day in late July was sitting in a car, stuck in heavy traffic, <u>heading north on the M1</u>. Cars towing trailers and caravans clogged the lane in front, almost bringing it to a
5 standstill. Holiday traffic. But <u>Josh was not going on holiday</u>. He was being <u>driven away from his friends</u>, his summer, <u>kidnapped by his own mother</u>.

2 So what are they going to do? Work? Help? Hide?

4 Really, or is he just moaning?

3 Why? When will he see them again?

3 Work in pairs. Read a bit more of the story, below. Decide what you think might be going to happen. Use the notes to help you.

> going where?
> mum doing what?
> what can Josh do?
> who does he meet?
> what happens – to mum?
>   – to Josh?

He glanced over to the driver's seat, where his mother sat, her face frowning and tense, her fingers drumming the steering wheel. It was hot in here, and stuffy. The car was packed with gear. They were going to …

Taken from *Truth or Dare* by Celia Rees

4 Next work on your own. Write about what you think might be going to happen in this story. Use these sentence starters to help you.

> Josh is being taken to . . .
> When they get there . . .
> After a little while . . .

5 Work as a class. Share what you have written.

1 Talk about:
   • where you agree as a class
   • where you have different ideas.
2 Explain how you came up with your ideas.
3 Learn the meaning of the key term below.

Key term

predict – to guess what will happen next based on what you know

Making sense of a text

This section will help you to:
• make sense of a text (infer and deduce meanings)
• read between the lines
• talk about your ideas and develop them
• answer questions with reasons

1   Work as a class. Talk about a story, film or TV programme where you guessed what was going to happen. How did you manage to guess right?

2   Work as a class. Sometimes you have to work out what is going on in a story. Read the story opening on the opposite page. Then do the work below.

> **1**   Read these sentences. Which one goes under which heading in the chart below?
>
>   • Mandy wears glasses.
>   • Mandy is being bullied.

Deduction *(What I can work out definitely)*	**Inference** *(What I can guess about what is going on)*

3   Work in pairs. Copy the chart above and read the following sentences. For each one:

> **1**   Decide if it is definitely true (deduction) or a good guess (inference).
> **2**   Write the sentence under one heading.
>   • This happens outside school.
>   • The teachers don't know about the bullying.
>   • The other girls have been waiting to get Mandy.
>   • Mandy wears sandals.

Outside the school gates

I saw them the moment I turned the corner. They were halfway down, waiting near the bus stop. Melanie, Sarah and Kim. Kim, the worst of all.

I didn't know what to do: I took a step forward, my sandal
5 sticking to the pavement.

They were nudging each other. They'd spotted me.

I couldn't see that far, even with my glasses, but I knew Kim would have that great big smile on her face.

I stood still. I looked over my shoulder. Perhaps I could
10 run back to school? I'd hung around for ages already. Maybe they'd locked the playground gates? But perhaps one of the teachers would still be there? I could pretend I had a stomach ache or something and then maybe I'd get a lift in their car?

15 'Look at Mandy! She's going to go rushing back to school. *Baby*!' Kim yelled.

1 Writers like to make you guess what is going on. They hope you will read on to find if your guesses were correct.

2 We can work out that Mandy definitely wears glasses.

3 We can guess that Melanie, Sarah and Kim have been bullying Mandy.

Taken from *Bad Girls* by Jacqueline Wilson

4 **Work on your own. Put these sentences in your chart.**

- It happens after school has finished for the day.
- The bullying has been going on for some time.
- Kim is the worst bully.

5 **Work as a class.**

1 Talk about how you decided where to put things in your chart.
2 What made you feel that some things were definite? Why did other things seem to be simply good guesses?
3 Learn what the key terms below mean.

Key terms

deduction – what you can work out from what you have read
inference – what you can reasonably guess to be true from what you have read

3 Understanding fiction

3.1

How the narrator feels

This section will help you to:
- understand the point of view of the person telling the story (the narrator)
- get a sense of the feelings of the characters
- think about the meanings of unknown words

1 **Work as a class. Read Cherie's problem. What help can you give her?**

> CHERIE: Sometimes when I am reading a text, there is a word I don't understand. What should I do?

1 Brainstorm what you can do when you read a word you don't know. For example:

> - *You can look a word up in a dictionary. Most words are in there, but not all.*
> - *You can often get an idea of what a word means from the words around it.*

2 Read the phrases below. You will meet them again later. How can you work out what the underlined words mean?

1 The capital letter tells you it may be a place. Do you think it is a big place? Why?

'a knot in my guts the size of <u>Tasmania</u>'

'cheese and <u>devon</u> sandwiches'

2 How can you guess that devon is a type of food and not a place?

Tasmania is an island off the coast of Australia and devon is a type of sausage. But you can still make sense of the text if you don't know that.

2

Work as a class. This is the opening of a story about a girl who has just moved school. Read it together. Then answer the questions.

IW
p.185

My first day

I'm so dumb.

I never thought I'd say that about myself, but after what I've just done I deserve it.

How could I have messed up my first day here so totally and completely?

5 Two hours ago, when I walked into this school for the first time, the sun was shining, the birds were singing and, apart from a knot in my guts the size of Tasmania, life was great.

10 Now here I am, locked in the stationery cupboard.

Just me, a pile of examination papers and what smells like one of last year's cheese and devon sandwiches.

What can you work out about the setting? Search text for key words, for example: school

Taken from *Blabbermouth* by Morris Gleitzman

1 Talk about a time when something went badly wrong for a friend.
- What happened?
- How did you feel?

2 Search the text. What can you work out about the setting?
- at home? at school?
- in Great Britain? in Australia?
- in a toilet? in a cupboard?
- How did you work out the setting?

3 How is the narrator feeling?
- relaxed? tense?
- clever? stupid?
- in control? lost it?
- How did you work out the narrator's feelings?

Key terms

setting – where a story takes place
narrator – the person telling the story

3 Work in pairs. Choose *four* words from the box below that best describe how the narrator is feeling.

nervous	silly	surprised
scared	shy	shocked
frustrated	foolish	childish
clumsy	crazy	shaken

1 On your own, put the four words in order. Put the best word first.

2 Explain to your partner why you put your words in that order.

4 Work on your own. For each word you chose, write a sentence that shows how the narrator might be feeling. For example:

surprised   I was surprised at just how quickly I
             had made a mess of things.

5 Work as a class. Share some of your sentences. Discuss what might have happened to make the narrator feel like this.

How characters feel

This section will help you to:
- understand how characters feel
- develop your drama techniques by acting in different roles

1 Work as a class.

1 The narrator of the extract on page 23 is called Rowena Batts. She was born with parts of her throat missing so she can't speak. Talk about what problems you might have if you were not able to speak.

2 Read 'What has happened so far', and the next part of the story, below. Answer the questions around the text.

What has happened so far

Rowena used to go to a special school which closed down. Her first day at an ordinary school starts well. She writes an introduction about herself because she can't speak. That is a success. Her new class are curious about her but seem quite friendly.

When the teacher is called outside for a minute, a boy called Darryn teases her. She ignores him when he calls her a freak. But when he starts on her parents, Rowena flips. Darryn is cleaning the frog tank. This is what Rowena does.

p. 184

2 What do you think the other students are thinking?

Rowena flips

1 What might Rowena be thinking and feeling? For example, 'I've blown it, now.'

I leapt across the room and snatched the frog Darryn Peck was holding and squeezed his cheeks hard so his red lips popped open and stuffed the frog into his mouth and grabbed the sticky tape from the art table and wound
5 it round and round his head till there was none left.

The others all stared at me, mouths open, horrified. Then they quickly closed their mouths.

3 What might the teacher think when she comes back?

Taken from *Blabbermouth* by Morris Gleitzman

What happened next
That is when Rowena goes and locks herself in the cupboard.

2 Work as a class. Use the notes and questions below to work out what the characters might be feeling (empathise with them).

1 Ask yourself: what might this character think or feel now?

2 Check: why might the character think or feel this?

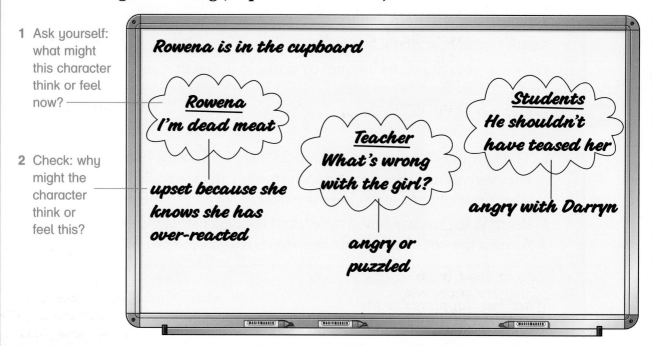

Rowena is in the cupboard

Rowena
I'm dead meat

upset because she knows she has over-reacted

Teacher
What's wrong with the girl?

angry or puzzled

Students
He shouldn't have teased her

angry with Darryn

1 Think about each character in turn. Write down as many ideas as you can in three minutes.
2 Talk about how the characters might feel.
3 Decide together which are the most likely reactions.

3 Work in threes.

1 Decide which of you will be:
   • the teacher trying to get Rowena to unlock the door
   • a student who wants to help Rowena
   • Rowena (who can react but does not speak).
2 Talk about what the teacher and the student might say (their dialogue). Talk about how they might behave.
3 Talk about how Rowena might react on the other side of the door.

4 Work in threes. Try out your ideas.

1 Act out what happens.
2 Change roles and play the other parts.
3 Who plays which part best? Why?

5 **Tell the class what worked well. Share your best dialogues with each other.**

1 Talk about what is good about them.
2 Make a class spider diagram like the one below. Use it to show the ideas that worked best when you acted the scene.
3 Add any new ideas you have when you are writing.
4 How did doing some acting help you to understand the characters' feelings?

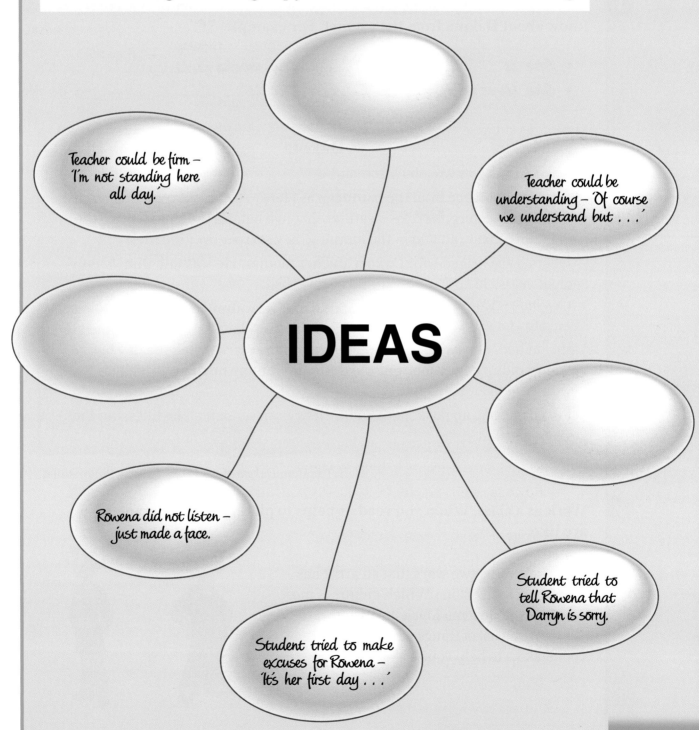

Teacher could be firm – 'I'm not standing here all day.'

Teacher could be understanding – 'Of course we understand but . . .'

IDEAS

Rowena did not listen – just made a face.

Student tried to tell Rowena that Darryn is sorry.

Student tried to make excuses for Rowena – 'It's her first day . . .'

Responding to characters

This section will help you to:
- think about two different characters
- say what you know about them and what you imagine them to be like

1 Work as a class. Read this passage together. Then brainstorm all that you know about Dakota from the extract. For example:

- *She is _____ old.*
- *She lives with _____ .*
- *She works _____ .*
- *She is _____ .*

Dakota

Dakota Pink was woken by screaming.

The screams came from the bathroom as Henry saw the silverfish. Silverfish are the tiny caterpillar-like creatures that live behind the sink. During the night they come out and in the morning they scarper over the tiles.

5 Henry Twig lodged with Dakota and her mother. He was tall, thin, twenty-eight years old and … very afraid of silverfish.

Usually Dakota, who was ten years old and very afraid of nothing, would get up and clear away the silverfish. But today, Sunday, she was determined to stay in bed. She had been working hard on the market stall the day before.

10 Henry didn't have a job. The most strenuous thing he did was pick his teeth with a golden toothpick.

I'm not getting up, Dakota thought. Henry can scream all he likes, but I'm staying in bed.

Taken from *Dakota of the White Flats* by Philip Ridley

IW
p.181

2 Work as a class. When you read, it helps to picture what characters are like.

1 Look at the two ways that an artist has imagined Dakota. Which picture is most like you imagined Dakota? Why? Use the list of things you know about Dakota to help you.

2 Write a profile of Dakota Pink. Use the Profile Box below to help you.

PROFILE

Name: _____

Age: _____

What this person looks like (size, height, face, hair, clothes, shoes):

_____

What they do: _____

How they behave: _____

How they talk: _____

WS 3

3.2

3 **Work in pairs. Re-read the passage and do the work below.**

1 Brainstorm everything you know about Henry Twig.
2 Talk about what he might look like.

4 **Work on your own. Write a profile of Henry Twig. Use the information you talked about.**

- There are some clues in the passage, but use your imagination as well.
- Use a Profile Box like the one above.
- Try to say *eight to ten* things about him.

5 **Work as a class.**

1 Share your ideas about Henry Twig. Talk about:
  - what he might look like
  - how he might speak.
2 How do you go about working out what a character is like?

4 Describing characters

This unit will help you to:
- understand how writers describe characters
- use description, actions and dialogue to show what a character is like
- draft your work

4.1 Understanding characters

This section will help you to:
- understand how writers show what a character is like
- think about the meanings of words

1 Work as a class. How can a writer show what characters are like? First read the Remember box. Then brainstorm different clues writers can give readers.

> **Remember**
>
> To work out what the writer is telling you about a character, you should:
> 1 Look at the words the writer used.
> 2 Then ask yourself:
>   - What do I definitely know from this?
>   - What else can I work out or guess?

Clues that writers give readers
- *what characters look like*
-

2 Work as a class. Find out how to understand a character in a story.

1 Read text **A** and the notes opposite. Then copy and complete labels 2 and 4 about Mr Berkhoff.
2 Read text **B**. What else does it tell you about Mr Berkhoff? Note your ideas in a chart like this.

	Definitely know	Reasonably guess
What Mr Berkhoff looks like		
What Mr Berkhoff does		
How he makes Ian feel		

Mr Berkhoff

A

Ian is in Mr Berkhoff's maths lesson.

1 Look for his **name**.

'Berkhoff' makes him sound hard.

IW
p.182

2 Look for **what he says and how he says it**:

His words show that

_____

_____

3 Look for **how he behaves**.

This shows Mr Berkhoff is feeling very angry.

4 Look for **how he makes others feel**.

People feel

_____

5 Look for **what he looks like**.

This shows he's huge and fierce like an angry bull ready to squash Ian.

Mr Berkhoff gives a bloodcurdling roar. He chucks his bit of chalk at the back wall, charges from the blackboard to the front desk and bellows, 'That is enough!'

5   Dead silence. The bit of chalk is rolling across the floor somewhere. I'm terrified to breathe because I'm sitting in the front row with Berkhoff's enormous gut jammed up against my desk twenty centimetres from my eyes. I don't dare look upwards. He'll be
10   frowning so hard his eyebrows will have merged into one thick black wavy line. He'll also be glaring around to see who chucked the pen top.

B

Mr Berkhoff is huge. He's tall and fat with a permanent scowl. He's sarcastic and he picks on people. He looks as if he could rip up phone directories with his bare hands.
5   He looks as if he could rip up kids with his bare hands.

Taken from *Rude Health* by Linda Aronson

WS 3
4.1

Work in pairs. Read all the instructions. Then do the work.

1 Read the description of Sister Gribble below. Stop each time you reach a break, and ask yourself:
  • What do I know?
  • What can I guess?

2 Do you agree with the thought bubbles? Why?

Sister Gribble

On Monday I went to the nursing home where they kept Grandad. I had to wait for ages in this little room which had hard chairs and smelt of stuff you clean toilets with. The nurse in charge wore a
5 badge which said, SISTER GRIBBLE.

1 I'm looking at her name.
The nurse is a sister so she is important. When you say her name it sounds quite fierce. She might be scary.

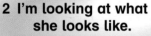

She had mean eyes. They looked like the slits on money boxes which take things in but never give anything back. She had her hair done up in a tight bun and her shoes were so clean you could see the
10 reflection of her knobbly knees in them.

2 I'm looking at what she looks like.
Sister Gribble is pretty. She looks like a kind and generous person. She is smart and tidy.

'Follow me, lad,' said the nurse after ages and ages. She led me down a corridor and into a small room. 'Before you go in,' she said, 'I want you to know one thing. Whenever the old man talks about
15 things that are not really there, you must say, "There's no such thing." You are not to pretend you believe him.'

3 I'm looking at how she speaks, what she says, and how she behaves.
Sister Gribble is bossy. She doesn't want to walk with him and chat.

I didn't know what she was talking about, but I did know one thing – she shouldn't have called
20 Grandad 'the old man'. He had a name just like everyone else.

4 I'm looking at how she makes others feel.
The grandson thinks Sister Gribble is doing a good job. She really seems to care about how he and his Grandad feel.

Taken from *There's No Such Thing* by Paul Jennings

4 **Work on your own.**

1 List the *five* clues you should look for to find out what a character is like.
2 Which *two* questions help you work out what a writer is saying about a character?

5 **Work as a class. Read how a famous writer called Charles Dickens described a man called Bounderby. Then do the work below.**

1 Search for clues and work out what Bounderby is like.
2 Bounderby thinks he is wonderful. Do you think Dickens agrees with him? How can you tell?

Mr Bounderby

He was a rich man; banker, merchant, manufacturer and what not. A big, loud man, with a metallic stare and a metallic laugh. A man made out of a coarse material, which seemed to have been stretched to make so much
5 of him. A man with a great puffed head and forehead, swelled veins in his temples and such a strained skin to his face that it seemed to hold his eyes open and lift his eyebrows up. A man with a **pervading** appearance on him of being inflated like a balloon and ready to start.
10 A man who could never sufficiently **vaunt** himself a self-made man. A man who was always **proclaiming**, through that brassy speaking trumpet voice of his, his old ignorance and his old poverty.

… He had not much hair. One might have fancied he
15 had talked it off; and that what was left, all standing up in disorder, was in that condition from being constantly blown about by his windy boastfulness.

A semi-colon tells readers to pause. Here, it helps emphasise the words 'talked it off' and how talkative Bounderby is.

Taken from *Hard Times* by Charles Dickens

pervading – all the way through him
vaunt – boast
proclaiming – boasting

4.2

Describing a character's looks

1 **Work as a class.**

1 Take it in turns to choose an adjective from the box below. Act out the word without speaking.

2 When you guess what word is being acted out, give a reason, for example, *The word is 'happy' because he is smiling.*

angry	happy	sad	shy	enthusiastic
calm	tired	scared	worried	proud

2 **Work as a class. In a story, how a person looks can tell you a lot about what they are like. Read the description of Mr Cobbett (Ian's head teacher). Then do the work below.**

Mr Cobbett

I'm in the Principal's room. Mr Cobbett, the Principal, is striding angrily up and down. His hands are clamped behind his back. He's tall and thin with a pointed nose, poppy eyes and an
5 Adam's apple so big and sharp-looking you'd think it would cut him. Cobbett is a big black crow.

Taken from *Rude Health* by Linda Aronson

1 What is Mr Cobbett like? How do you know?

2 Read the flowchart opposite. It shows you one way to work out how to describe someone. Use it to work out what a happy person might look like.

Step 1 Decide what kind of person he or she is:

angry	(happy)	sad	shy	enthusiastic
calm	tired	scared	worried	proud

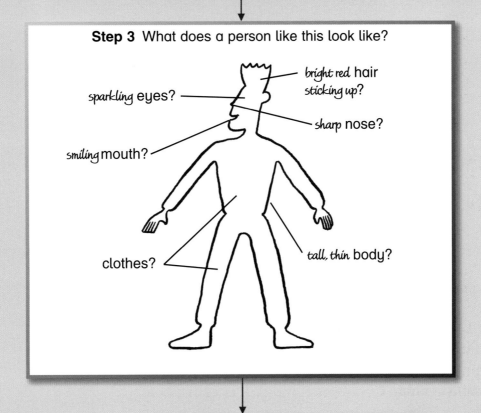

Step 2 What animal is this kind of person most like?

Step 3 What does a person like this look like?

bright red hair sticking up?

sparkling eyes?

sharp nose?

smiling mouth?

clothes?

tall, thin body?

Step 4 Make up a good name for this sort of person.

e.g. *cheerful Milly Giggle*   *proud Cecil Highborn*

3 **Work in pairs. Make up a new English teacher.**

> **1** Use the flowchart on the previous page to help you describe this character.
> **2** Make sure both of you jot down the ideas.

4 **Work on your own. Use your notes. Write a paragraph describing your character. Start like this:**

I stared at my new English teacher _____(name)_____.
_____ had _____.

_____ reminded me of _____.

5 **Work with a different partner.**

> **1** Read each other's descriptions.
> **2** Tell your partner why you chose those adjectives to describe your character.

4.3 Writing about what a character does

This section will help you to:
- describe actions
- show what a character is like
- choose the best words for your writing

1 **Play this game as a class.**

1 Make a list of different feelings. Start with:

sad, happy, jealous ...

2 Now make a list of *ten* different actions. Start with:

running, playing video games, cooking dinner ...

3 Take turns to choose an action and a feeling. Then mime doing the action as if you are in that mood.

4 The rest of the class must guess the action and the mood. The first person to guess chooses the next words to act out.

2 **Work as a class. Read the texts on the next page. Then answer these questions.**

1 a What is Ned feeling? Which actions did the writer use to show you this?
  b What other clues are there about what Ned is like?

2 a What is Mum feeling? Which actions show you this?
  b What other clues are there about what Mum is like?

3 In text **B**, why is 'flung' a better word to use than 'threw'?

Ned

A

Ned is waiting for Mum to come home.

1 A character's actions show what he or she is like.

He cooked up two-minute noodles, <u>hacked off</u> a slab of cheese and <u>emptied the tin</u> of Milo into a litre of milk.

2 The way the person does the action shows what they are feeling.

5 Ned had a pile of homework – maths, English, science – but at seven o'clock he was still watching TV; half listening, waiting, annoyed now. At himself. At her. At everything.

B

Mum has come home and Ned will not turn the television off.

1 'Swung' is better than 'walked'. It shows how fast she's moving.

10 Suddenly, like a **berserk** ten-pin bowler, she **swung** in from the kitchen with the cast iron frying pan and **flung** it at the screen with all her might.

2 'Berserk' is better than 'mad' because it's a stronger word.

Taken from *Remote Man* by Elizabeth Honey

berserk – totally mad, wild

3 Work in pairs.

1 Read the remember box.

> **Remember**
> You can show what a person is like by carefully choosing:
> - action words (**verb phrases**):
>   *giggled   was afraid   moaned   roared   went crazy*
> - words which tell you how the action was done (**adverbs**):
>   *suddenly   slowly*

2 Copy and complete the text below. Use words and phrases that show Chong is shy and nervous. Choose words from the box below or use your own.

The loud music told Chong this was where the party was. He
_____ on the door and _____. At once the door burst
open. 'Hi! You got here!' shouted Polly. Chong _____ into the
dark hallway. 'Hello,' he _____. Then he _____ and
stopped. Chong _____ .

thumped	crept in	tapped	strode in	shuffled
waited	shouted	mumbled	went red	quietly
grinned	wished he hadn't come		felt excited	nervously

4 Work on your own. Write a paragraph about one of these characters:

- The English teacher you made up in section 2 activity 3 (page 36) – describe what your character does and says when a student uses a mobile phone in class.
- Ned – describe how he does the washing up after tea. He is still annoyed with Mum.

5 Work as a class. Listen to each other's descriptions. Pick out the actions that show what the character is like.

Writing speech

This section will help you to:
- write a conversation (dialogue) that shows what characters are like
- punctuate speech in longer sentences

1 **Work as a class.**

    1 What do you already know about punctuating speech?

    2 How can you show readers the way people speak? Make a list of words and phrases you can use instead of 'said'. Start with:

> *yelled, whispered softly . . .*

    3 Take it in turns to choose one of the ways of speaking in your list. Say the sentence below in that way. The rest of the class has to guess how you are saying it.

> *'I'm going shopping with my mum.'*

2 **Work as a class. Read the text opposite. It shows you how to write a conversation. Then answer the questions.**

    1 List *three* ways Mike speaks. What is he like?

    2 What is Dominic doing? What kind of person is he?

    3 Look carefully at the labels telling you how to write speech.

    4 It's the next day and Dominic is back again. Read the speech below and answer these questions.

       a How should it be written out?

       b Why is it important to put the words of each speaker on a new line?

> Back again, Mike smiled. Dominic said, Mum forgot her sandwiches today. Every day she forgets something.

Only joking

Dominic is talking to Mike, the security guard at the place where his Mum works.

'So what brings you to our neck of the woods?'
Mike smiled.

'Mum forgot her key card.'

5   'I know.' Mike sighed. 'I had to issue her with a temporary one for the day.'

'She'd forget her teeth if she didn't keep them in a glass by her bed,' I told Mike. 'She sees them as soon as she wakes up each morning and yet sometimes I have to remind her that

10   she's about to leave the house with only her gums on show!'

Mike stared at me. 'Your mum has false teeth?!'

I burst out laughing. 'You won't tell her I told you that, will you?'

Mike gave me a **wry** look verging on disapproval. 'I should

15   have known this was another of your wind-ups!'

1 Each time Mike and Dominic speak, their words go on a new line.

2 The spoken words begin and end with a speech mark.

3 The punctuation goes inside the speech mark.

wry – slightly amused

Taken from *Dangerous Reality* by Malorie Blackman

3 **Work in pairs.**

1 Dominic enjoys winding Mike up. What other things could he say about Mum's bad memory that Mike might just believe? For example:
She locked the car keys in her car, leaving the engine running …

2 Act out the conversation between Mike and Dominic.

4 **Work on your own. Write out the conversation you made up.**
You can only use 'said' once. Remember to:

• put each speaker's words on a new line   • use speech marks.

5 **Work in pairs. Read each other's conversations.**

1 Does each speech begin on a new line? Put // to show where any new lines are needed.

2 Tick each speech mark that is in the right place.

5 Staging scripts

5.1

This unit will help you to:
- respond to playscripts
- develop how you write and stage a playscript
- explore character by acting
- work with others

Responding to scripts

This section will help you to:
- give a response to a playscript
- understand how characters are shown in playscripts
- explore the action in a play

1 Work as a class. Plays tell different stories, but they often show you what happens when people disagree with each other (conflict).

> **1** Think of situations where you hear one person disagreeing with another.
> **2** What are the disagreements about?

2 Work as a class. Read the disagreement opposite. It starts a play called *End of the Road*. The notes show what one class thought about it.

> **1** Answer the questions in blue.
> **2** How far do you agree with the class?

3 Work in pairs. Take the roles of Grandad and Sandy. Try out the scene in more than one way. For example:

• Grandad being very grumpy	• Sandy trying to be polite
• Grandad being just a bit difficult	• Sandy being very cheerful

Home from work

The scene is the kitchen. It is the end of the day. Grandad is reading a newspaper. He does not seem to be in a good mood. He seems annoyed by the breakfast dishes still on the kitchen table.

5 *We hear the front door open and shut. GRANDAD doesn't look up. SANDY enters and he pointedly continues reading.*

SANDY: Hi, Grandad.

GRANDAD: Oh, it's you. Where's your mother and father?

SANDY: Still at the café. It's been murder.
10   On the go all day.

GRANDAD *(sour)* That makes a change.

SANDY   *(taking off coat)* Here, I saw you out back talking to old Miss Hemsley.

Taken from *End of the Road* by Kara May

1 Why does Grandad keep on reading?

2 How is he treating Sandy?

3 How does he look?

4 Is he pleased or sarcastic?

5 Is Sandy responding to his bad mood or ignoring it?

Notes: What the class thought

Grandad — rude
- he ignores Sandy at first
- Sandy's been working, not him
- we think the sides of his mouth are turned down
- he's looking for a row

Sandy — making an effort
- ignores his rudeness
- tries to make conversation
- trying to cheer him up
- not yet picked up on his mood

4 Work in pairs. Read below what Sandy and Grandad say a little later in the script, and the notes. You are going to act it out. Do this work.

> **1** Talk about Sandy. How will you play the part? Make notes.
>
> **2** How will you play the part of Grandad? Make notes.
>
> **3** Try acting out the script.
>
> • Try to make the characters sound real.
>
> • Make sure the words can be heard clearly.
>
> • Can you improve the way you play the characters?

Whose TV?

SANDY: I'm going to the front room. It's time for my series.

GRANDAD: You can't watch that.

SANDY: You're not going to bed already! — **1** Is Sandy surprised or annoyed?
5   I suppose I could move the telly in here, into the kitchen.

GRANDAD: I'm not going to bed. I'm watching snooker.

SANDY: But it's my series! — **2** Sulking or angry?

GRANDAD: You've got your whole life to be watching these
10   series of yours.

SANDY: But Grandad, I told you this morning — **3** Confused or frustrated?
              I wanted to watch it.

GRANDAD: And I'm telling you I'm watching snooker. I'm entitled to watch a bit of telly at my age. Not
15   much to ask.

SANDY: I come back specially to watch it. It's not fair.

GRANDAD: Instead of watching telly, you should be giving your mother a hand, get that washing up done.
20   It's been there since breakfast. I don't know what sort of house this is.

SANDY: I've been working at the café since eight this morning. So's Mum and Dad. — **4** Is Sandy appealing to Grandad or angry with him?

GRANDAD: You don't know what work is.
25   *(Going)* Young people, you've no idea.

Taken from *End of the Road* by Kara May

5 Work as a class. Talk about your performances.

1 What did you like about them? For example:

> The way Sandy sounds cheerful but Grandad sounds grumpy

2 What could you improve? For example:

> louder … slower … Make Grandad sound sarcastic

Developing the characters

This section will help you to:
- develop characters in role
- create your own piece of drama

1 Work as a class. Talk about the two characters you have been working on: Sandy and Grandad. What have you learned about them?

2 Work as a class. This is how a group built a piece of drama. It was about how Sandy and Grandad might treat each other next day. Do the work below.

1 Read the students' ideas below. Which do you agree with?
2 Read the scene the group made up. Talk about how their ideas appear in the script.
3 How have the students made the opening believable?
4 How have the students made a strong ending?

'We thought Sandy should be making an effort but have a bit of a temper.' **Pat**

'I wanted Grandad to become more helpful, but the others thought he should stay miserable.' **Jamie**

GRANDAD:	So you're helping today.	
SANDY:	I help every day. In the café and here. It's not easy, you know.	
GRANDAD:	At your age, my child, I worked twelve hours a day with twenty minutes for lunch. There were no coffee breaks every half hour in my time.	5
SANDY:	You should come down the café and see just what hard work it is.	
GRANDAD:	You should just get on with the dishes.	
SANDY:	And you should think about helping a bit yourself. Getting old is no excuse for letting everyone run around for you.	10
GRANDAD:	I've never been spoken to like that in all my life.	
SANDY:	That's probably why you've become so lazy . . . and rude.	15
GRANDAD:	Just you wait till your father comes in.	

'Why should Sandy put up with Grandad? He shouldn't get away with it just because he's old.' **Amir**

'I wanted to make them both sound tired.' **Lee**

3 **Work in groups of four to make up a scene.**

> **1** Choose a situation about which Sandy and Grandad might disagree.
> For example, Grandad complains that:
> - Sandy doesn't eat proper food
> - Sandy's bedroom is a mess
> - Sandy comes in late at night and wakes him up
> - Sandy plays awful music and it's too loud.
>
> **2** What do you want Sandy and Grandad to be like?
> **3** What sorts of things might they talk about?

4 **Split each group into two pairs. Each pair must work out the scene. One of you is Sandy, the other is Grandad.**

> **1** Work out the first few lines of your scene. If you are not happy with it,
> try a different opening.
> - Try to make it sound believable.
> - Think of a good ending to the scene.
>
> **2** Work as a group again. Watch each other's scenes. Who has produced:
> - good openings?
> - believable characters?
> - strong endings?

5 **Work as a class. Report back on what your pairs did. What worked well? What didn't? Why?**

Understanding characters

This section will help you to:
- understand characters by acting in role
- create a monologue for a character

Key terms

dialogue – characters speaking to each other
monologue – one person speaking on their own

1 **As a class, talk about Grandad.**

1 This is what we know about Grandad.
  - He is staying in the same house as his grandchild.
  - He has a bed in the front room where the television is.
  - He is not getting on well with Sandy.

  How could these three things be connected?

2 **Work as a class. A group of students talked about what Grandad might think and feel. They made up the monologue opposite. Read it aloud, then do the work below.**

1 The students made these comments. Which two are most important?
  A Grandad is jealous of Sandy.
  B Television is all Grandad's got left, and he doesn't even think much of that.
  C Grandad is angry at how he's been treated.
  D Grandad feels like a thing, not a person.
  E Grandad knows he is being difficult.

2 Which three words fit Grandad best?

dull	bored	frightened	puzzled
angry	awkward	miserable	ungrateful

3 a Get one person to perform his speech quietly, sitting down.
  b Try it again standing up and being more aggressive.
  c Which works better?

Grandad's speech

It's all right for Sandy: there's a whole life still to be lived. What have I got left? A couple of years in front of a television being bored silly by stupid repeats. That's if I'm lucky. I didn't ask to come here. They just shoved me out of the hospital and into their car. No one consulted me. The doctors talked to my daughter, they even talked to my son-in-law, but they told me nothing. For all I know I could be dead in two weeks. Not that anyone would care. They just get on with running their blasted café and leave me here like a piece of furniture nobody needs any more.

I wanted to go home. So what if I couldn't cope? At least I'd be in a mess in my own place. Here, I'm not in a mess, I *am* the mess. I'm taking up a room they need, I'm taking up time they haven't got and I'm making it worse every time I speak.

I don't expect people to understand. I thought I might get a bit of respect but that doesn't happen these days. If you're old, you're useless. Past your sell-by date and ready to be dumped in the bin.

1 Only Grandad speaks.

2 He says what he really thinks and feels.

WS 3
5.1

Now talk in pairs about Sandy. Answer the questions.

1 a Where does Sandy work?

   b Who does Sandy argue with, and why?

   c What does Sandy feel is unfair?

   d What else would you say about the character?

2 Which of these words describe Sandy?

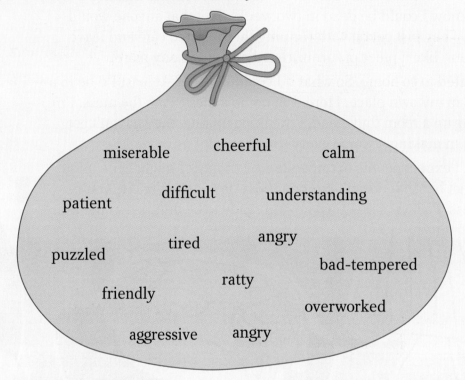

miserable   cheerful   calm

patient   difficult   understanding

puzzled   tired   angry

friendly   ratty   bad-tempered

overworked

aggressive   angry

3 How might Sandy talk to an audience if he or she was alone on stage?

4 Work on your own. Make up a monologue for Sandy.

1 Decide what Sandy might say about the situation with Grandad.

2 Read the script starters opposite. You may want to use one of them to begin your monologue.

5 Work as a class. Listen to each other's monologues. Say what is good about each performance. For example:

It's easy to follow Sandy's thoughts.

You find out what Sandy really thinks and feels.

It was clear and loud enough.

Sandy: I know he doesn't mean to be difficult but he drives me . . .

Sandy: It was all right until he came. Mum, Dad and me were getting on fine. The café was going OK. We were one happy family. Then he . . .

Sandy: If it wasn't such hard work at the café, I think we'd all get along . . .

Sandy: I like him really. I try my best to cheer him up. It's just that . . .

Sandy: The problem's having him in the front room. It used to be a place to relax. Now he's taken over . . .

Sandy: I work. He doesn't. Even if he's ill, he could do a bit. Instead he . . .

5.4 Writing a script

This section will help you to:
- write your own script
- make your characters come alive

1 Work as a class. Remember how Grandad behaved when Sandy came home from work (page 43). Describe how people in your family behave when they are in a bad mood.

2 Work as a class. Read the handwritten script on the opposite page. Then do the work below.

5.2

1. Find the name of someone who is speaking.
   - Where is the name? Is it on the left or the right?
   - Is it in capitals or lower case letters?
2. Find *three* stage directions (words that tell actors what to do and how to speak).
3. How has the writer shown which words are stage directions?

3 Work in pairs. Imagine you come home and someone in your family is in a bad mood. Talk to your partner about what you and that person might say.

4 Work in pairs.

5.2

1. On your own, write a script based on what you have talked about.
2. Check your partner's script.
   - Is it clear who is speaking?
   - Are there any stage directions? If so, are they clear?
3. Perform the scripts in pairs.
   - Can you improve your script?
   - Make any changes you think are needed.

5 Share your scripts as a class.

1. Which ones are good?
2. What must you remember when you write a script?

<u>*The scene is the living room. Mum is picking up magazines.*</u>

MUM   It's always a mess.

ME   (<u>coming in</u>) Evening, Mum.

MUM   You're late.

ME   Ten minutes.

MUM   You're always late.

ME   Not always.

MUM   (<u>raising her voice</u>) Don't argue with me!

1 This is the first stage direction.

2 Exclamation marks are used to:
 • show words are shouted: 'Stop!'
 • make a strong point: 'You are in big trouble!'

3 The apostrophe shows where a letter has been left out: do + not = don't (the 'o' in 'not' has been missed out).

6 Choosing words for poetry

6.1 Writing descriptions

This section will help you to:
- write descriptively
- work together on ideas

1 Work as a class. Talk about the best poem you have heard or read in the past year. Say what you like about poetry.

2 As a class, read the poem 'The Thingy' on the opposite page.

1 Choose your favourite line. Say why you chose it.
2 Read these two-word descriptions. What animal is being described?
   - Ear twitcher
   - Tail wagger
   - Leg sniffer.
3 Make up a two-word description for:
   - a fish
   - a snake
   - a mouse
   - a pet of your own.

The Thingy

Shin kicker

Snot flicker

Crisp muncher

Shoulder huncher

5 Grudge bearer

Out starer

Back stabber

Biscuit grabber

Sock smeller

10 Fib teller

Thinks that it's

Uri Geller.

Loud belcher

Slug squelcher

15 Pillow drooler

I'm the ruler

Gonna beat yer

That'll teach yer

Bog ugly

20 Swamp creature

Found mainly

Undercover

What is it?

MY BROTHER!

Lindsay MacRae

1 The poem is mainly made up of two-word descriptions.

2 Each line tells you one thing about The Thingy.

3 What do you think the poet means when she calls him a 'grudge bearer' and an 'out starer'?

Work in pairs. A head teacher described himself using two-word descriptions. They have been jumbled up in the box below.

1 Write out the words.

2 Link them up in pairs to make the best two-word descriptions of a head teacher. The first link has been done for you.

Parent	tracker
Number	talker
Trouble	signer
Tough	checker
Cheque	pleaser

WS 4

6.2

Work on your own. Describe yourself using two-word descriptions.

1 Use some or all of the words below. Put a new word in front of each of them. For example:

maker ————→ mess maker

looker	————→	_____ looker
drinker	————→	_____ drinker
reader	————→	_____ reader
watcher	————→	_____ watcher
eater	————→	_____ eater
fighter	————→	_____ fighter
footballer	————→	_____ footballer
dreamer	————→	_____ dreamer
hater	————→	_____ hater
thinker	————→	_____ thinker

2 Choose your *three* best descriptions.

5 Share your best descriptions with the whole class. As you listen, pick out the best description. Say why you like it. For example:

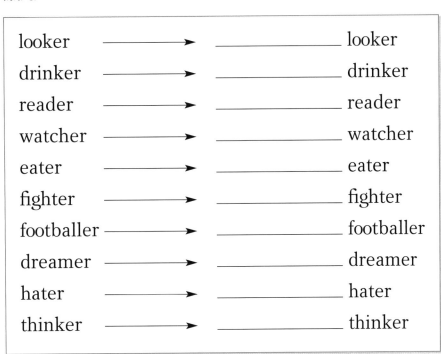

It really suits him!

I like the sound of …

… made me laugh.

6.2 Looking at rhymes

> **This section will help you to:**
> - check that you understand about rhyme
> - write rhyming poetry

1 Work as a class. Brainstorm what you know about rhyme. Make up some examples, like these:

> *toast/post*   *rip/grip*

2 Work as a class. Most of the lines in 'The Thingy' end in –er, but there's more to rhymes than that. Find out how rhyme really works. Read the first six lines again, then answer the questions.

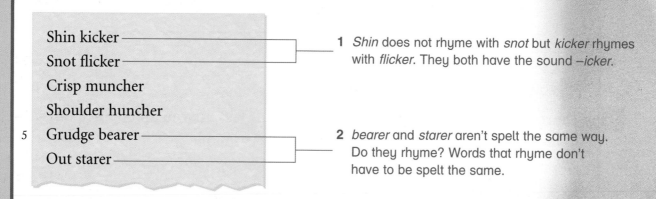

Shin kicker
Snot flicker
Crisp muncher
Shoulder huncher
5 Grudge bearer
Out starer

1 *Shin* does not rhyme with *snot* but *kicker* rhymes with *flicker*. They both have the sound –*icker*.

2 *bearer* and *starer* aren't spelt the same way. Do they rhyme? Words that rhyme don't have to be spelt the same.

1 What other words end in –*icker*?
2 Which of these three words rhymes with *starer*?
- fairer
- poorer
- nearer.

3 **Work with a partner. Read the phrases below.**

1 Find *ten* pairs that rhyme.
2 Choose the *three* rhymes you like best.
3 Look back at the Key term box on page 55. Find three phrases on this page that use alliteration.

Worst trier

Playground fighter

Second rater

Gossip bearer

Toast griller

Strange creature

Best liar

Nose picker

Time filler

Crisp cruncher

Secret sharer

Money stealer

Mud flicker

New beginner

Story writer

Mice muncher

Biggest squealer

Soccer hater

Final winner

Head teacher

WS 4
6.3

Work on your own. Write a rhyme about someone. Choose a person you know or make someone up.

1 Choose *one* of the pairs of rhyming words from the opposite page.

2 Think of a word to go before each of the words. For example:

> Bone crusher
> Big blusher

or

> Can crusher
> Red blusher

3 Write your own poem of *eight to twelve* lines. Use the rhyming words opposite or add in your own ideas for rhymes.

Remember
If you don't know some of the words opposite, use a dictionary to find out what they mean.

5 **Share your poems with the class. Choose a favourite pair of lines that rhyme in each poem you hear. Say why you liked them. For example:**

> I think … was a clever rhyme because …

> I also thought the use of alliteration in … worked well because …

> I also laughed at the choice of words that were linked together because …

6.3 Choosing and using words carefully

This section will help you to:
- create a poem about sounds
- think about the effect of the words you choose
- use words carefully and well
- use a thesaurus

1 Work as a class. There are lots of words you can use for sounds. You can find them linked together in a book called a thesaurus.

1 Read the 'sound' words opposite. Think of at least three more soft sounds and three more loud sounds.

2 Some words can be used for both soft *and* loud sounds, for example: *clink, clunk, hiss*.

Think of at least three more words that could be used for a soft *or* loud sound.

Key term

thesaurus – a book which brings together words that are linked. For example:
- all the words for *things* (nouns), like:

room	bathroom, bedroom, lounge, study, toilet

- all the words for types of *feelings* (adjectives), like:

happy	bright, cheerful, glad, joyful, lucky, merry, pleased, smiling, sunny

sad	blue, depressed, down, glum, homesick, hurt, low, miserable, unhappy, upset

- all the words that you could use instead of *said*. For example:

answered, commented, declared, exclaimed, remarked, repeated, replied, reported, stated, suggested

Soft sounds ... from a thesaurus

creak	squeak	chatter
clink	whisper	tick
thud	whistle	hoot
swish	murmur	grunt
sizzle	hum	scratch
sigh	plop	purr
buzz	clunk	rumble
tap	tinkle	ring

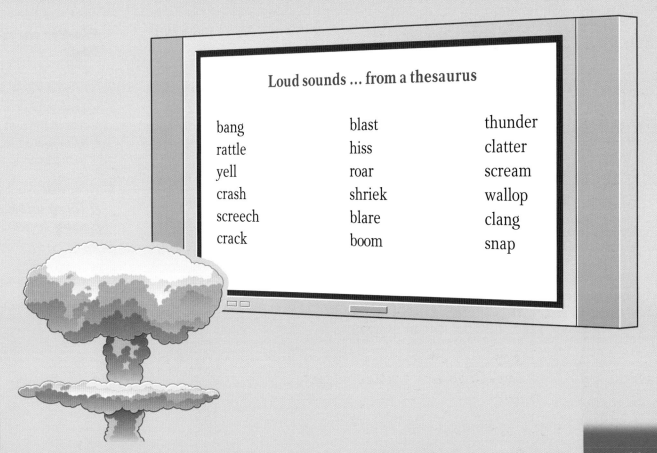

Loud sounds ... from a thesaurus

bang	blast	thunder
rattle	hiss	clatter
yell	roar	scream
crash	shriek	wallop
screech	blare	clang
crack	boom	snap

2 Work as a class. Find out how you can use sound in your own writing. Read the poem below. Then do this work.

1 List *three* sound words the writer used.

2 Could the poet really hear the page talking?

3 What could you hear in your classroom if you had Super Power hearing? Write down your ideas, for example:

- *someone else's thoughts*
- *the sunlight falling . . .*

It was …

It was so silent that I heard
My thoughts rustle
like leaves in a paperbag …

It was so peaceful that I heard
5 the trees ease off their coats of bark …

It was so still that I sensed
a raindrop's shiver
at the groan of the paving stones
as they muscled each other for space …

10 It was so silent that I heard
the page of a book
whispering to its neighbour
'Look, he's peering at us again …'

Pie Corbett

1 Leaves and paper bags make a rustling sound. What else rustles?
Plastic carrier bags . . .

2 Notice all the 's' sounds.
- How many can you find in the first stanza?
- Where are they used in the second stanza?

3 What else might groan?
A lorry with a heavy load . . .

4 What else whispers?

3 **Work in pairs. You are going to write a sound poem.**

1 Read aloud the title and opening lines for the four stanzas.

> ### In the room
>
> It was so silent that I heard
>
> ....
>
> It was so peaceful that I heard
>
> ....
>
> It was so still that I sensed
>
> ....
>
> It was so silent that I heard
>
> ....

2 Decide where the room is. It could be in school, at home or even in your dreams.

3 Decide what sounds you can hear that you will describe in each stanza. The sounds can be real or imaginary. Make a plan like this:

Stanza	Sound	Description
1		
2		

4 Write the first stanza of your poem. Use some of the words you read on page 63.

5 Work with another pair. Talk about your lines and any ways you can improve them.

4 **Now work on your own. Write the rest of your poem.**

5 **Work as a class.**

1 Share your best lines with the rest of the class.

2 Make a class poem using the best lines from everyone's poems.

7 Exploring setting and mood

This unit will help you to:
- understand a description of a place
- write your own description of a place
- understand how a mood is created
- write a description that creates a mood

7.1 Understanding descriptions of places

This section will help you to:
- understand the clues a writer gives you when describing setting

Key term

setting – where a story takes place. A writer might describe the sights, sounds, smells, and what might be tasted or touched.

1 Work as a class. Writers tell readers about the setting by giving them clues. What clues could a writer give to show what each of these places is like?

- a market

> *smell of fish, stall-holders shouting out . . .*

- a busy part of a city

> *cars roaring, people rushing . . .*

2 Work as a class. Find out how to work out what a description tells you about a place.

1 Read text A, opposite. Then read the notes and chart which explore the clues in the first sentence.

2 What does the second sentence show you about this setting? Use a chart like the one shown, to help you.

East London

A

It was a hot sticky night and East London was alive.

Every car stereo was turned to the full, every
convertible car was converted and every house that had
a fan was burning up electricity.

1 Look for clues about what the place is like.

2 Look at the words the writer chose. Work out what you can reasonably guess.

3 You can collect the clues in a chart like this one.

definitely know	can reasonably guess
East London	
hot sticky night	it's summer
alive	it's a busy area

4 The things you can reasonably guess are what the words *suggest*.

WS 3

7.1

Work in pairs.

1 Look at the highlighted clues **1–5** in the text below. Talk about what they suggest about East London.

2 Note your ideas in a chart like the one above.

B

Every fifteen minutes or so sirens could be heard
in the distance – and some not so distant.

   People took it for granted that whatever was
going down had nothing to do with them. All they

5 had to do was get out of the way and stay
composed as they did so.

   Even the police looked relaxed tonight: those
that were on the cruise had their windows down,
shirtsleeves up and radios blasting out – police

10 radio that is, talk radio.

1

2

3

4

5

Taken from *Face* by Benjamin Zephaniah

Work in pairs.

1 Read the text below.

2 Pick out *five* clues that tell you what the place is like.

3 Explain what each clue suggests.

4 Make a note of your answers in a chart like the one below.

definitely know	can reasonably guess
1 The market is jumbly and untidy	A busy place with lots of different kinds of people and things
2 You never know what you are going to find	
3	

IW

p.183

The market

The market where Dad works is all jumbly and untidy and that makes it exciting. And you never quite know what you are going to find. There's everything there – old books, masks and jokes,
5 toys, cheeses, fish, jewellery, hats – and of course my dad with his clocks and watches. The stall holders aren't in uniform either, like they are in the supermarket. They wear what they like. In winter they're all bundled up in coats and scarves
10 or layers of jerseys because it can get very cold in the market. That's because the roof's made of glass. You can look up and see clouds floating by and pigeons looking down at you. Anyway the *feeling* in the market isn't cold. It's warm and
15 friendly and comforting.

Taken from *Minders* by Diana Hendry

5 ## Work as a class.

1 Share what you found out about the market described above. How did you work out your answers?

2 Explain to a partner what a setting is.

7.2

Describing a setting

> **This section will help you to:**
> - describe a setting

1 Work as a class. The fish and chip shop shown on the next page is the setting for a story. You are going to describe it. Plan your ideas first.

> **1** Brainstorm different things you can see, hear, smell, taste and touch in a fish and chip shop. Note your ideas on a spider diagram like this.

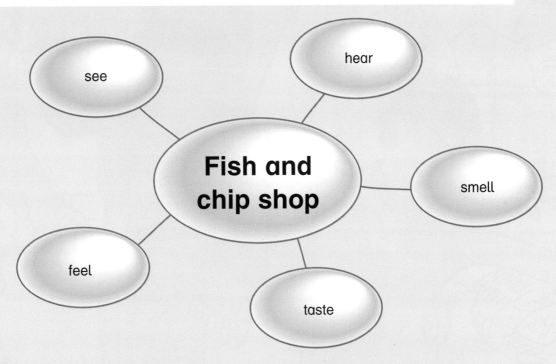

2 Work as a class. Read the text below. It shows you how to work on a description. You can try out different adjectives (describing words).

Step 1 Write a sentence. ——— It was hot.

Step 2 Write it two or three more times. Each time try to put in more description.
It was very hot and crowded.
It was very hot and crowded and it smelt of oil.

Step 3 Choose which sentence to use in your best copy.

> **1** Which sentence would you use in your best copy? Why?

3

Work in pairs. What might you _hear_ in a fish and chip shop like the one opposite?

1 Work out _four_ good sentences describing the sounds. You must be able to use them in your best copy. Choose words from these boxes to help you, and use your own.

A

Nouns				
boys	girls	man	woman	chips
fryer	salt shaker	paper	till	door

B

Adjectives					
chatting	laughing	hissing	crackle	rustle	patter
pop	whoosh	sizzle	ting	creak	chink

4

Work on your own.

1 Describe the setting of a story which takes place in a fish and chip shop. You can start like this:

> I walked through the door and I . . . (saw? heard? smelt?)

2 Use your best sentences from activity 3. Work out and use some other good describing sentences.

5

Work as a class. Share how you worked out which were your best sentences.

1 What sentence did you start with?
2 How did you change it? Why?

Understanding mood

This section will help you to:
- understand how writers create a sense of mood
- think about the effects of different types of sentences

1 **Work as a class.**

1 Have you ever been in a place that seemed:
- creepy?
- sad?
- exciting?

2 What was the place like? Describe it to your class.

2 **Work as a class. Read the three paragraphs on the next page. Each has a different mood. Work out why the mood is different in each paragraph.**

1 For each highlighted word ask yourself:
- What does it mean?
- What does it suggest?

2 Make a note of your ideas in a chart like the one below.

Words	What they mean	What they suggest
great days	*days that he enjoyed*	*the family were happy*

Key term

mood – the feeling attached to a place or a situation

Changes

We had some great days on the water. We'd go out when it was rough, when no one else would, and we'd go skimming over the waves, **exhilarating** in the speed of it, in the sheer joy of it. And if there wasn't a breath of wind, we didn't mind that either. Sometimes we'd be the only boat on the whole **reservoir**. We'd just sit and fish instead – by the way, I was better at fishing than either of them – and our dog, Stella Artois, would be curled up behind us in the boat, bored with the whole thing, because there was no one to bark at.

Then the letter arrived. Stella Artois savaged it as it came through the letterbox. There were puncture holes in it and it was damp, but we could read enough. The brickworks were going to close down. They were both being made **redundant**.

There was a terrible silence at the breakfast table that morning. After that we never went sailing on Sundays any more. I didn't have to ask why not. They both tried to find other jobs, but there was nothing.

Taken from *Kensuke's Kingdom* by Michael Morpurgo

1 The words in red make the mood happy.
The words in blue make the mood sadder.

2 Using longer sentences makes it feel carefree.

3 Using shorter sentences makes it feel more tense.

exhilarating – feeling liveliness and joy
reservoir – lake used for water supply
redundant – losing their jobs

3 **Work in pairs. Read the text below. Pick out and explain:**

> **1** *two* words which show the mood is unhappy
> **2** *two* actions that show the father is unhappy
> **3** *one* shorter sentence that makes it feel more tense.

Unemployed

A creeping misery came over the house. Sometimes I'd come home and they just wouldn't be speaking. They'd argue a lot, about little niggly things – and they had never been like that. My father stopped fixing things
5   around the house. He was scarcely ever home anyway. If he wasn't looking for a job, he'd be down in the pub. When he was home he'd just sit there flicking through endless yachting magazines and saying nothing.

Taken from *Kensuke's Kingdom* by Michael Morpurgo

4 **Work on your own. Write *five* sentences like the one below. Explain how the writer of the paragraph above built an unhappy mood.**

> The mood is unhappy because the writer used the (word/action/sentence)
> _____ which suggests _____.

5 **Work as a class.**

> **1** Listen to each other's sentences. Do you agree with them?
> **2** Explain what mood is.

7.4 | Creating a mood

This section will help you to:

- draft a text with readers and purpose in mind
- choose which sorts of sentences to write
- choose words to create an effect

1 Work as a class. Read the text below. Answer the questions.

Firework night

Gary is watching fireworks. He is standing by the bonfire.
Gary enjoyed watching the yellow and red flames bright against the dark sky and he listened to the happy crackle of the dry wood burning.

1 Is the mood happy or sad? How can you tell?
2 What do these words mean:
   - mood
   - setting?
3 How many sentences are there in the text?
4 Share what you know about writing in sentences.

2   **Work as a class. In 'Firework night', the writer wrote one long sentence.**

1 Why do you think the writer chose a long sentence? How did she want the reader to feel? *Happy, angry, tense, excited …*

2 Read the steps below. It shows you one way to build longer sentences in your own writing.

> **Step 1**
> Think of two ways of describing something, such as smoke.
> **The smoke looked like clouds of candyfloss. It smelt sweet.**

> **Step 2**
> Use one of these connectives to join the two sentences:
>   and   or   but
> **The smoke looked like clouds of candyfloss and it smelt sweet.**

> **Step 3**
> Check that your longer sentence still makes sense!

3   **Work in pairs. You are going to write *four* longer sentences that describe the fireworks opposite really well. Keep the mood happy.**

> **Key term**
>
> **connective** – a word that joins two sentences together: *and, or, but*

1 Use the phrases in each box below to make *two* short sentences that describe what is happening. Write them out.
For example: *A rocket shot brightly into the black velvet sky. It soon disappeared like a magic trick.*

> | A rocket shot …   It soon disappeared … |
> |---|

> | The Catherine Wheel spun …   Sparks shot … |
> |---|

> | Gary's favourite firework …   Perhaps the best was … |
> |---|

> | Balls of light flew …   They were the colours of … |
> |---|

2 Join the pairs of sentences together using one of these connectives:
    and   *or*   *but*

3 Write out the longer sentences. For example: *A rocket shot brightly into the black velvet sky but it soon disappeared like a magic trick.*

4 Work on your own. Gary is eating a burger and chips. Use the phrases in the box below to help you write *three* more long sentences.

- Describe the food carefully. Choose words that show what it looked, smelt and tasted like.
- Remember to make the mood happy.
- Use these connectives: *and*   *or*   *but*

He grabbed the …	he munched …	He smiled at …
he licked …	The smell of …	he thought of …

5 Share your description with the rest of the class.

1 Listen to other people's descriptions.
2 Pick out a sentence that is really effective at describing the food and creating a happy mood.
3 Explain which words make it work so well.

8 Exploring an older poem

This unit will help you to:
• study a poem from a different time
• understand a ballad's key features
• discuss and develop your ideas

8.1

What makes a ballad?

> **This section will help you to:**
> • explore the ballad form
> • find the key features of a ballad
> • scan a text to answer a question

1 **Work as a class.**

> **1** Think of the words of your favourite songs. Do any of them tell a story? What kinds of story do they tell?
>
> **2** Read the explanation box below.

> **Explanation**
> Many early poems were songs that told a story. They are called **ballads**.
>
> We do not know who wrote these ballads. They used rhyme and repetition to make the poem easy to remember. People learned them from each other. Each person could make changes to the words.

2 **Work as a class. 'How comes that blood?' on page 80 is a song. It is over one hundred years old. Read it together.**

> **1** What is the first question in the poem?
>
> **2** What is the first answer?
>
> **3** Find the next *two* excuses the son gives for the blood on his shirt.
>
> **4** Look at the fourth stanza. What has the son done?
>
> **5** Read to the end of the poem. How do you know that the son is afraid of what might happen?

Work in pairs.

1 Read the chart below of things you often find in ballads.

Things you often find in ballads	Example
Repeated lines	'How comes that blood all over your shirt?' (lines 1 and 13)
Words that rhyme at the ends of lines	'me' and 'be' (lines 2 and 4)
Questions and answers	'How comes that blood all over your shirt?' (line 1) 'It's the blood of my little guinea pig' (line 3)

2 Scan the poem and find another example of each. Read the key term box to help you.

3 Make a note of your answers in a chart like the one above.

Key term

scan – When you scan a text, you know what you are looking for. Your eyes move quickly over the text until you find it. You look out for key words or features to help you find what you want. For example, you have been asked to look for words that rhyme at the end of lines in the poem on page 80. You should:

1 **Spot the main thing in the question you have been asked**.
Here, it is 'words that rhyme' at 'ends of lines'.

2 **Decide where to look**. Here, you only need to look at the ends of lines.

3 **Run your finger along the text as you search for the answer**. Here, run your finger down the last word of each line, only. Note down the words that rhyme.

4 **Work on your own. Do the work below. Make a note of the line numbers to talk about your answers later.**

1 Find *two* lines that show you that this is a poem about families.

2 Find *two* lines that show you that this is a poem about death.

3 Find *two* lines that show you that this is a poem about fear.

5 **Work as a class. Read the ballad aloud again.**

1 One person can be the mother. Another person can be the son.

2 Try to make it sound as if the son is making excuses.

3 As you read, remember what you have learned. Where might the son sound most afraid? Where might you want to emphasise the rhyme?

4 Talk about what you expect a ballad to have in it.

How comes that blood?

"How comes that blood all over your shirt?
My son, come tell it to me."
"It's the blood of my little guinea pig –
O mother, please let me be."

5   "Your guinea pig's blood is not so red.
My son, come tell it to me."
"It's the blood of my little hunting dog
That played in the field for me…"

"Your dog lies **yonder**, O my son,
10   And this it could not be."
"It is the blood of my old **roan** horse
That pulled the plough for me…"

"How comes that blood all over your shirt?
My son, you must tell to me."
15   "It's the blood of my little brother Bill
Who I killed in the field today…"

"And what will you do when your father comes home?
My son, come tell it to me."
"I'll put my feet in the bottom of a boat
20   And sail across the sea."

yonder – over there
roan – speckled with white

8.2

Why we read older poems

This section will help you to:
- explore why some older poems are still read today
- understand ballad form by creating your own verses

1 Work as a class. Tell the story of the ballad 'How comes that blood?' on page 80. Then answer these questions.

> **1** Do people still say *yonder* and *How comes*? What do they say instead?
>
> **2** Which of these are in the ballad:
> - a family argument
> - a parent who keeps asking questions
> - a murder?
>
> Do they still happen today?
>
> **3** What do you expect a poem that is a ballad to be like?

2 Work as a class. Below is a modern version of the ballad. The third line is missing. Read the poem then answer the questions.

> ### A modern ballad
>
> How come you've trashed your new trainers?
> Nathan, explain that to me.
>
> ....
> So it's not my fault, you see.

1 Who might be asking this question?

2 Who do you think is speaking here?

> **1** Which of these three lines would you use to complete the verse?
>
> **A** We all played rugby in the mud
>
> **B** My brain won't work
>
> **C** They sent us running in the rain
>
> **2** Look at the chart of 'things you often find in ballads' on page 79. Which can you find in this verse? Give examples.

WS 3

8.2

Work in pairs to make a four-line verse out of these five lines.

1 Move the lines around so that the verse makes sense.
2 Get rid of *one* line.

> Gary knows what happened,
>
> Nathan, just tell me how.
>
> That's all I can say for now.
>
> I ate three buttons for my lunch,
>
> How come you've ripped your new school shirt?

WS 4
8.2

Work on your own.

1 Put these lines in the right order.

> *And wouldn't let it go.*
>
> *The dog was playing catch with me*
>
> *How come you've lost your English book?*
>
> *Nathan, I need to know.*

2 Write out and finish this verse for the ballad.

> *How come you've lost your tie again?*
>
> *.......... what's going on?*
>
> *...*
>
> *So it isn't .... that's wrong.*

WS 5
8.3

Work as a class. Put together the verses you have been working on in this section. You've got your own class ballad! Now look at it together.

1 Give it a title.
2 What things does it contain that you often find in ballads?

8.3 Developing good ideas

This section will help you to:
- play a part in discussions
- work together to develop the best ideas

1 **Work as a class.**

1 Later you are going to work in groups. First, decide what is important when you are talking about something in a group. Choose from the following and add your own ideas:

- shout loudly at all times
- listen carefully
- take it in turns to speak
- don't interrupt
- keep to the point
- don't let *everyone* say something

2 Talk about the ballad 'How comes that blood?' on page 80. Was it about:

- animals
- boats
- excuses?

Explain why you think that.

2 **Work as a class. You are going to work out a story about excuses for being late home. Your story will *begin* with some of the excuses below. Read them and do this work.**

1 Come up with some more excuses of your own.

2 Write up the best of those excuses.

3 Talk about how your parents reply to excuses.

Excuses

Question: 'How come you're home so late from school?'

Possible answers:
- My teacher forgot to let us out.
- The bus was late.
- I stopped to help an old lady who was unwell.
- I was helping the science teacher clean out the gerbil's cage.
- I fell asleep in English and no one bothered to wake me up.
- I went to an after-school maths lesson for those who are extra keen.

1 Who do you think is asking this question?

2 Who do you think is answering?

3 Which is your favourite excuse?

3 Work in a group of three. Your story will *end* with one of the explanations below.

1 Read the explanations below of what really happened.

2 Work on your own. Choose the explanation you like best. You are going to argue that the group should use this one in the story. To support your argument you will need:

- good reasons for your choice

- reasons for why the other explanations aren't as good

- careful choice of words and the way you say them, to persuade others that your choice is best.

3 Work as a group. Talk about and decide which explanation is best, and why.

What really happened

A I came out of the showers and found that my clothes had been stolen. I stood in a towel while the PE teacher went searching. The cleaners all laughed at me.

B The head teacher was interviewing me about the theft of a large hairy spider from the biology lab. He eventually found it … in my pocket.

C I was teasing the caretaker's dog when it bit at my trousers and made a large hole at the back. I had to sit in a caretaker's coat while the hole was stitched up.

4 Now work in your group of three, as if you are a film crew.

1 Choose which of you will be:
- the son or daughter
- the mother or father
- the film director who offers support and advice.

The director will report back to the class on how it went.

2 Together, work out your story which includes:
- a question and an excuse – use some of the ones you talked about earlier in activity **2** on page 85
- a reaction from the parent who does not believe it
- more excuses and reactions
- a final explanation of what really happened – use the one you agreed on page 86.

3 Perform your final story.
- **The mother or father** should think carefully about *how* they ask the question and react to excuses. What words will they emphasise? What tone of voice will they use? How will they stand and how will they look?
- **The son or daughter** should think carefully about *how* they give their excuses. What attitude will they take – angry, loud, quiet, funny? How will they make their excuses sound real?
- **The director** should offer advice. In what ways might the words spoken, tones of voice, and behaviour between the parent and child work better?

5 Work as a class.

1 The directors report back to the class on how the story was performed. They should say:
- what worked well
- how the storytelling could be improved.

2 Work as a class. Talk about how easy it was to work in a group. Work out a list of rules for talking in groups. The ideas below will help you get started.

- *Take it in turns to ...*
- *Listen to ... and don't ...*
- *Keep to the ...*
- *Make sure everyone ...*

3 Share three main things you have learned about ballads and storytelling.

9 Recounting events

9.1

This unit will help you to:
- recount events
- speak and write formally
- speak and write informally
- play different roles

Recounting a scary event

This section will help you to:
- give a spoken recount of an exciting event
- use the past tense and time link words

1 Work in pairs. What happened in the last episode of your favourite soap opera? Tell your partner.

2 Work as a class. Listen to your teacher read Arif's spoken recount below. Then answer the questions.

1 What is Arif talking about?
2 What makes this a recount?

1 The **verbs** are in the past tense.

2 **Time link words** show the order in which things happened.

When I was in Year 7, I went on a trip with the school to a theme park. At the end of the day, a really scary thing happened. I was on my way back to the coach, late. At first, I heard this huge bang. Then I looked up and saw smoke and flames. A gas bottle had blown up or something. Next, my friend grabbed me. We just ran and ran and ran. Finally, we got back to the coach, puffing and panting. The teachers were really pleased to see us at first. They thought we were in the fire. Then they had us for being late!

3 **Work in pairs.**

1 Read the sentences below. Put them in order to finish Arif's recount. Start like this:

The sentence order is: D, _____.

A Then he shouted at us.

B Later, we got back to school and the head teacher wanted to see us.

C Finally, he banned us from school trips for being late!

D On the coach, the teacher phoned the head teacher on her mobile.

E Next, he phoned our parents.

F At first, he smiled.

2 Think of something exciting, unusual or scary that happened to you. Tell your partner what happened.

- Use time link words like these:

first	next	later
then	finally	

- Use past tense verbs in your recount, such as:

looked	stayed	came	went	saw

WS **4** **Work on your own.**

9.1

1 Now write out the first three sentences of your recount. Remember to use the past tense and time link words.

2 When you have finished, underline all past tense verbs in one colour. Underline all time link words in another colour.

5 **Work as a class. What do you need to remember to do when you are writing a recount?**

Formal and informal English

This section will help you to:
- use informal and formal English
- role play in different situations

1 **Work as a class.**

> **1** What is a recount text?
>
> **2** What verb tense do you use in a recount text?
>
> **3** List as many time link words as you can.
>
> **4** Read the key terms box below. Then read the two recounts opposite.
>
> **5** Talk about these two questions:
>
> > **a** How do you know they are both recounts?
> >
> > **b** How are the two versions different?

Key terms

informal English – how you speak to friends or family
formal English – how you speak to the head teacher or an adult you don't know well

2 **Work as a class. Look again at what Josh said to the Head of Year. Find formal phrases which mean the same as the informal phrases in the chart.**

Informal	Formal
kids	*students*
bags and stuff	
you could hear a pin drop	
dead loud	
Boy, was she in for a surprise!	

Josh was talking to a friend. This is what he said:

1 Many words and phrases are **informal**. Find more examples of informal words and phrases.

> I was taking my maths test, you know, in the big hall. All the kids' bags and stuff were at the front of the hall. At first, you could hear a pin drop. Then a mobile phone went off, it was dead loud. I went all hot – it was mine! Next the teacher began hunting in the bags. Finally, she got to mine. Boy, was she in for a surprise! My pet mouse was in a box in my bag. Next, she screamed blue murder as my mouse ran up her arm! In the end, everyone laughed so much the test had to stop. Later, I got into trouble with a capital T.

Then Josh talked to his Head of Year. This is what he said:

> I was taking my maths test. All the pupils' bags were at the front of the hall. At first, all the students worked in silence. Then my mobile phone rang really loudly. Next, the teacher tried to find the phone to turn it off. I knew what she would find. Then she found my bag and screamed when she opened it. My pet mouse was in a box in my bag. In the end, the test had to be stopped. I am very sorry.

2 Josh uses **formal** words and phrases.

3 Work in pairs on these two role plays. One of you is Person A. The other is Person B. Decide when to use formal English and when to use informal English.

> **Role play 1**
>
> **Person A** During break, you and a friend saw someone come into the library and steal a laptop computer. Answer another friend's questions about what happened.
>
> **Person B** Ask Person A some questions about what happened at break. Begin, '*Tell me about what happened at break.*'

> **Role play 2**
>
> **Person A** You are the head teacher. Ask Person B to recount what happened at break. Begin, '*What happened in the library at break?*'
>
> **Person B** You saw what happened at break in the library. You are talking to your head teacher. Answer her questions.

4 Work on your own. Finish these sentences.

- When you talk to your friend, you use ...
- When you speak to someone like your head teacher, you use ...

5 As a class, discuss the differences between formal and informal English.

Writing formal English

This section will help you to:
- use formal English in writing

1 **Work as a class. Discuss how you talk to different people.**

1 How do you talk to your friends and family?
2 How do you talk to your head teacher and other adults?
3 What are the differences?

2 **Work as a class. Read the incident form below. Then do the work.**

1 Find the features of a recount.
2 How can you tell this is formal writing?
3 Why should you use formal English for this type of writing?

Dawson Comprehensive School

Incident form

Date of incident: *18.7.02*

Place of incident: *Examination Hall*

Person reporting incident: *Ms P. Hollings (Head of Year 7)*

Pupil(s) involved in incident: *Joshua Peters*   Form: *7D*

Brief recount of incident:
Joshua was taking his mathematics test in the examinations hall with all the other Year 7 pupils. All the pupils' bags were at the front of the hall. At first, all the pupils worked in silence. Then a mobile phone rang loudly. Next, the teacher in charge, Ms Jones, tried to find the phone to switch it off. Finally, she found Joshua's bag and screamed when she opened it. Joshua's pet mouse was in a box in his bag and escaped. In the end, the test was stopped. Joshua was sent to me, his Head of Year.

Action:
His parents were informed and Joshua has been punished.

1 The teacher has used formal English words and phrases. Words are out in full and not abbreviated.

2 The passive voice is used in formal writing. For example, here the writer has used it instead of 'Ms Jones stopped the test'.

3 **Work in pairs.**

1 A student has begun to draft an incident form about the theft from the library. Look again at the role play on page 92 to remind yourself what happened.

2 Read the recount of the incident below. Find *two* sentences that are too informal.

Dawson Comprehensive School

Incident form

Date of incident: _____

Place of incident: _____

Person reporting incident: _____

Pupil(s) involved in incident: _____

Brief recount of incident:

I was mucking about in the library with my mate. Then we saw a man in his twenties enter the library. He looked a bit shifty. We didn't recognise him. He wasn't a teacher. At first, he ...

Action:

WS 4
9.3

Work on your own.

1 Rewrite the informal sentences turning them into formal English.

2 Copy and complete the incident form. Describe what happened next. Fill in all the details.
   • You can make up the information you need.
   • Remember to use formal English.

5 **With your partner, check your work.**

Have you:
• used formal English?
• used the past tense and time link words?
• started each sentence with a capital letter?
• finished each sentence with a full stop?

9.4 Differences between speech and writing

This section will help you to:
- recognise the differences between speech and writing
- role play different situations

1 Work as a class. What are the differences between speech and writing? List as many as you can.

2 Work as a class. A newspaper reporter interviewed two students about a theft at their school. Read the words of the interview on the next page. Then answer these questions.

1 How can you tell someone is speaking?
2 Why do we hesitate, repeat ourselves and use incomplete sentences when we are speaking?
3 What do the pronouns 'they' and 'one' refer to?

Interview

1 The name of the person who is speaking.

2 Repetition.

REPORTER: Can you tell me about how you caught the thief who took your school computer?

HANNAH: Yes ... well ... er ... it was, let me think, it was last Thursday. Me and my mate were down the market. We saw this bloke, didn't we? We recognised him straight away as the bloke who nicked the laptop.

10 **REPORTER:** Paul, tell me some more.

PAUL: We recognised him straight away. He was the ... it was the bloke we'd seen in our school library. He was flogging laptops and mobile phones. We asked him if they worked. He ... er ... he gave me one to try. It was well cool. So we, well Hannah ... rang the police on the mobile ...

HANNAH: ... and I told them to come and they did! They arrested him straight off!

3 The dots (called an ellipsis) show she is hesitating.

4 Unclear pronouns.

5 Incomplete sentences.

3 **Work in groups of three on this role play.**

> **Person A** is the interviewer who asks, '*What would be your dream come true?*'
>
> **Person B** answers the question.
>
> **Person C** listens carefully.

1 Repeat the role play three times so everyone has a turn at each role.

2 After each role play, discuss these questions. Did the speaker:
- hesitate
- repeat something
- say an incomplete sentence?

3 After all three role plays, work with another group. Talk about what you noticed.

4 **Work in pairs.**

1 Read this article. The reporter wrote it about Hannah and Paul.
2 Compare it with the words of the interview opposite.
3 Make a list of the changes the reporter made.

Use a table like the one below. Some entries have been filled in to help you.

Spoken English of interview	Written English of article
• Uses informal words such as 'bloke', …	• Uses formal words such as 'man', 'stole', 'selling' and …
•	• Uses complete sentences
• Uses some unclear pronouns – 'they' and 'one' could mean laptops or mobile phones	• Uses clear pronouns – 'one' refers to …
• An ellipsis (…) shows the speaker is hesitating	•
•	• There is no repetition
• The speaker uses 'fillers' such as 'er' and 'let me think'	•
•	•

COMPUTER KIDS CATCH THE THIEF!

Hannah and Paul, two pupils from Dawson Comprehensive School, caught the man who stole a laptop from their school library. They were in the market when they spotted the thief. He was selling
5 laptops and mobile phones.

Paul said, 'We asked him if the phones worked and he gave us one to try.'

Clever pupil, Hannah, phoned the police and reported the thief. The police came and arrested the
10 thief straight away.

5 **Work as a class. Compare your lists of changes the reporter made. Discuss the reasons for the changes.**

10 Finding information

This unit will help you to:
- learn to find information
- use an index and a contents page
- make notes

10.1

Where to look for information

This section will help you to:
- find the information you need

1 Work as a class. Here are some sources of information. Brainstorm as many others as you can.

Places	People
radio	*teachers*
library books	*classmates*
CD-ROMs	*parents*
Internet	*experts you know*

2 Work as a class. Read how four pupils reacted to the homework they were given. Talk about what the pupils say.

History teacher: Find out about life during the Second World War.

Pupil 1: I'm going to look on the Internet.

Pupil 2: I'm going to ask Gran.

1 There are lots of websites giving information about the Second World War.

Geography teacher: Find out about the local houses which were flooded last week.

Pupil 3: I'll look in last week's newspapers in the library.

Pupil 4: Who could I ask?

2 It is a good idea to look in last week's newspapers. Can you explain why?

3 Suggest who pupil 4 could talk to about the local houses.

3 **Work in pairs.**

1 Talk about where you would find information about:
  a Thomas Edison for a science project
  b Roald Dahl for an English lesson
  c wildlife programmes for your auntie
  d India for a geography project
  e electric fires for your grandad who wants to buy one.

4 **Work on your own.**

1 List *three* things you want to find out. They can be:
  • questions that come from school work
  • questions connected to things that interest you
  • anything you think is puzzling.
2 List where you would look for the answers.

5 **Work as a class. Share some of the questions you thought of.**

1 Does anyone know any of the answers?
2 Agree on the best way to find or check the answers.

10.2 Finding information in a book

> **This section will help you to:**
> - find the information you want in a book
> - use an index and a contents page
> - scan a text to find information

1 Work as a class. Some students want to find out when Dahl wrote *Matilda*. They have a book called *A Life of Roald Dahl*. Talk about how they can find the bit of the book that would tell them.

Key terms

scan – to look quickly through a text to find the information you need
key words – the words which tell you most about what you are working on

2 Work as a class. Look at the Contents page and Index opposite. Read and talk about the labels on the right-hand side. Do the work below.

    1 Which pages tell you about *Danny, the Champion of the World*?

    2 Where can you find out about Roald Dahl's childhood?

    3 'People are listed by their last name in an index.' True or false?

    4 Chapter 12 is a timeline. What sort of information might it give you?

Contents

- The **Contents** list is at the front of the book.
- It tells you the titles of the chapters.
- It gives you the page number that starts each chapter.

To use the Contents:

1 Scan the list of chapter titles.
2 Stop when you find a chapter that might have the right information.
3 Turn to the page.

For example, to find out how many children Roald Dahl had, try Chapter 6, 'Family life'.

Index

- The **Index** is at the back.
- It is alphabetical.
- It tells you on what page you will find information about the things listed.

To use the Index:

1 Find the key word in your question.
2 Scan the Index to find the first letter of your key word.
3 Run your finger down the Index till you find your word.

For example, to find out about Matilda, look under 'M'.

3 Work in pairs. Copy and complete these sentences. Use the Contents and Index on page 101.

> **A** Read about Roald Dahl's family in Chapter _____ .
>
> **B** Chapter 2 tells you about _____ .
>
> **C** To find out how he spent his day, read _____ .
>
> **D** Harald Dahl was Roald's _____ .
>
> **E** You will find out about *Boy* on pages _____ .

4 Work on your own. Use the Contents and Index on page 101. Is each of these statements true or false?

> **A** Some of Dahl's books have been made into films.
>
> **B** Dahl wrote a book called *James and the Enormous Crocodile*.
>
> **C** Roald Dahl won an award called the Whitworth Prize.
>
> **D** Walt Disney was interested in some of his writing.
>
> **E** Roald Dahl once lived in New York.

5 Work in pairs. Check each other's answers to activity 4. Afterwards, work as a class to discuss these questions.

> **1** What have you learned about finding information?
>
> **2** When do you think you would find a Contents list more useful than an Index?
>
> **3** When do you think you would find an Index more useful than a Contents list?

Making notes

> **This section will help you to:**
> - get information from paragraphs
> - record it in a form you can use
> - communicate information to others

1 **Work as a class.**

> 1 Brainstorm different ways to help yourself to remember information.
> 2 What do you know about writing notes?

WS 2 **Work as a class. Read this paragraph about spiders and see how a student made notes from it.**

10.1

This paragraph introduces spiders to the reader.

1 The **main point** is in the first sentence. It deals with what people know about these animals.

> Everyone knows what spiders look like, but what do we know about them? They are not insects. Insects have six legs. Spiders have eight legs. They belong to a family of animals called arachnids.

5

2 The **topic sentence** in a paragraph tells readers the main point.

3 The **detail** tells us that they have eight legs, and are arachnids, not insects.

Search the paragraph for key points, and make notes like this.

What we know

not insects

8 legs

arachnids

- Use few words.
- Don't write in sentences.
- Set out key points in a clear way.
- Make a list so it is easy to find each point.

Key term

key points – the important points or information that you need to know

Spiders!

Spiders are best known for spinning silk
webs. The silk comes from inside the spider
and it starts off as a thick liquid. The silk
can be squeezed out of two holes in the
5 back of the body. The moment that the
liquid hits the air, it dries into a thin line.

WS 3
10.1

**Work in pairs. Read the paragraph opposite about spiders.
Then do the work below.**

1 Decide how to finish these sentences.

   a This paragraph is about spiders making ...

   b The silk inside the spider's body is in the form of a ...

   c The silk comes out of ...

   d When the silk meets air it becomes a ...

2 Make notes about how spiders make their webs. This has been started for you below.

Making ....

silk inside ....

comes out ....

in air ....

Work on your own. A spider diagram is a way of recording notes. Copy out the one opposite. Do the work below to complete it.

1 a Read paragraph **A**, below.

b Find the key points.

c Complete section 3 on your spider diagram.

A

> One of the biggest spiders in the world is called the tarantula. It can grow to a length of 25 centimetres. It normally only comes out at night and can catch frogs and snakes as well as insects. Tarantulas are unusual because they are furry.

5

2 a Read paragraph **B**, below.

b Find the key points.

c Complete section 4 on your spider diagram.

B

> Spiders like to eat insects alive or just after they have killed them. They have fangs in their mouths and poison glands in their jaws. They use the fangs to inject poison into the insects they have caught. Then it's lunchtime!

5

3 Now complete section 2 on your spider diagram. You did the work you need for this in the activity on page 105.

5 **As a class, talk about the points below. Try to explain them.**

1 These diagrams are called spider diagrams even when they are not about spiders.

2 Students who make notes do better in exams than those who just read and don't make notes.

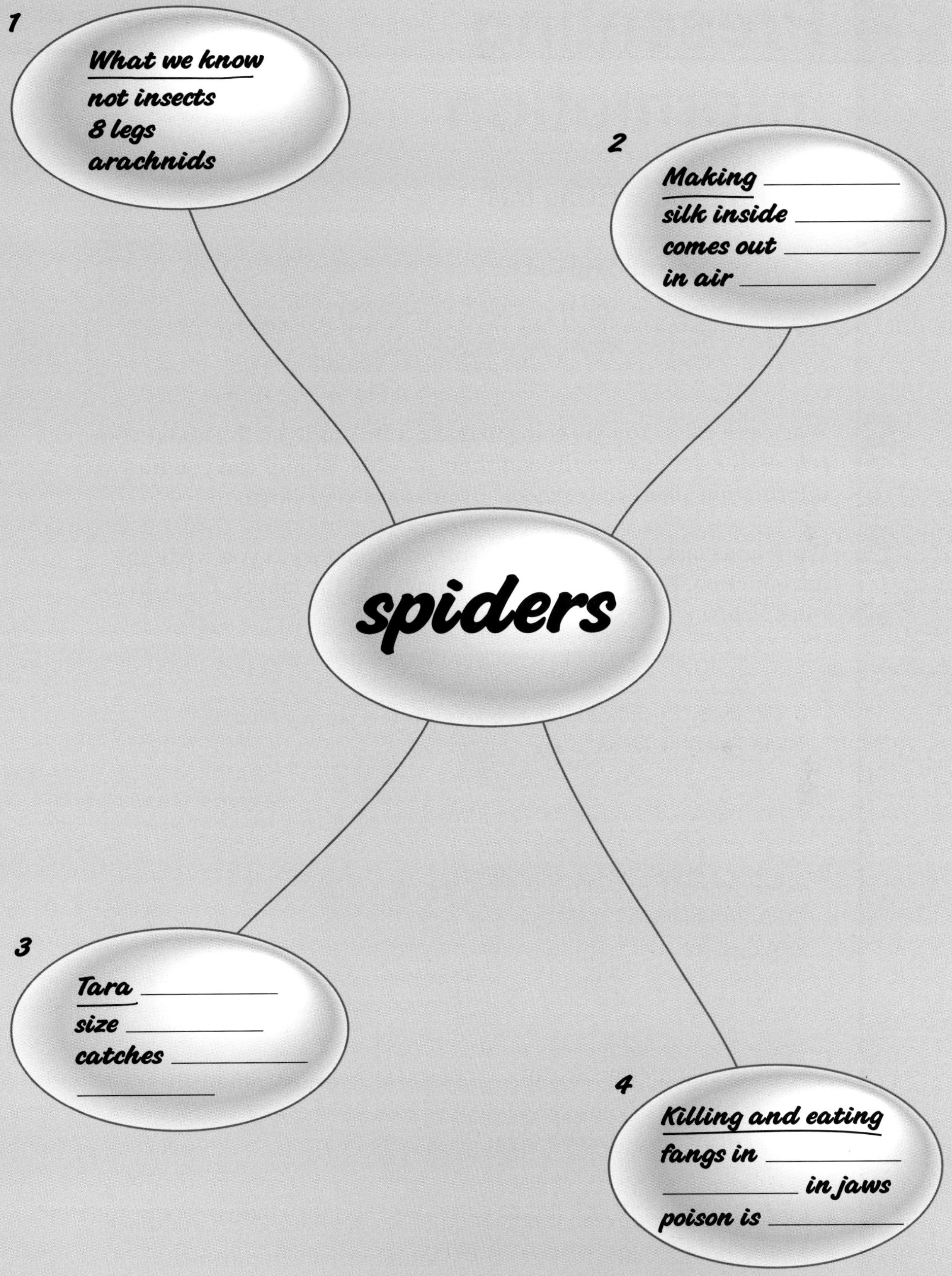

1

What we know
not insects
8 legs
arachnids

2

Making _____
silk inside _____
comes out _____
in air _____

spiders

3

Tara _____
size _____
catches _____
_____

4

Killing and eating
fangs in _____
_____ in jaws
poison is _____

11 Presenting information

This unit will help you to:
- plan and revise an information text
- think about who will read a text, and why
- present ideas in a suitable way

11.1 Who are you writing for?

This section will help you to:
- think about who will read your text, and why
- choose the right language for your reader

1 Work as a class. You are going to make a two-page leaflet about your school. It is for new pupils and their parents. Where can you find information about your school? Brainstorm your ideas.

2 Work as a class. Find out how to suit your readers as you write the introduction. Read these three openings and the labels. Then do the work below.

The introduction gives the reader a feel for what the school is like.

A
> Hi, we're Rushford High School and we want you to chill out and feel the welcome.

This sounds as if it is speaking to a young person. Which words make it sound chatty and friendly?

B
> Welcome to Rushford High School. We aim to make you feel that you can do your best with us.

This is the opening parents might expect. Can you explain why?

C
> Hi! Rushford here. School's our business. You want learning? You got it. We're the place that puts your head in gear.

Does this sound right for a school leaflet? Why not?

1 Who is meant to read your leaflet? (They are the leaflet's **audience**.)
2 What is the leaflet trying to do? (This is the leaflet's **purpose**.)
3 Choose the opening that suits your audience and purpose best. Write it down.

3 **Work in pairs. Talk about how each of these groups of sentences will sound to your audience. Choose the best for your leaflet and write it down.**

D We work together here. That's how we do it. Got it? You will when you join us.

E The key to our success is work. Lots of it. Listen. Do your best for us and you'll make it.

F The key to our achievement is working together. If you listen well, you will learn well. If you help others, they will help you.

4 **Now work on your own.**

1 Read these five sentences.
2 Choose *two or three* to add to your leaflet. Which ones are best for your audience.
3 Write them down.

G We hope you like our school – we certainly do.

H From the moment school starts until it finishes, there will always be plenty for you to do.

I We're a great bunch of people and we look forward to working with you.

J We hope you make the most of your time at Rushford.

K We want you to be proud of your school and we look forward to being proud of what you achieve.

5 **Work as a class. Listen to each other's introductions.**

1 Do they sound right? Why?

Because parents ... A leaflet has to ...

2 Could they be improved? Why? How?

Planning and writing a leaflet 1

This section will help you to:
- collect information
- organise your information
- set it out clearly and helpfully

1 Work as a class. It is important to give the reader the right information. Talk about what you needed to know on your first day at this school.

2 Work as a class. Look at the way the front page of the leaflet from Rushford High School is set out (the *layout*). Answer the questions around the text.

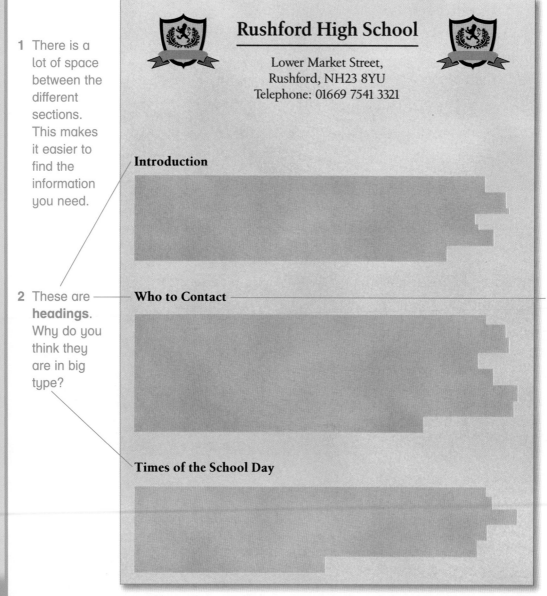

1 There is a lot of space between the different sections. This makes it easier to find the information you need.

2 These are **headings**. Why do you think they are in big type?

Rushford High School

Lower Market Street,
Rushford, NH23 8YU
Telephone: 01669 7541 3321

Introduction

Who to Contact

Times of the School Day

3 Why do you think the address is smaller than the name of the school?

4 The most important information goes on the front.

5 Who might be on this list? *Head teacher, Deputy Head, Head of Lower School …* Who else?

3 **Work in pairs.**

1 What are the names of the people to contact in your school? Make a list.

2 What are the important times in your school day? Make a list of the following:
- start time
- lesson times
- break times
- lunchtime
- end of school.

3 Choose the most important of these for your leaflet.

4 **Work on your own. Read the key terms box and then do the work below.**

1 Look carefully at the layout of the Rushford High School leaflet. Use the same layout for your own front page.

2 Write up your front page using these headings:
- Introduction
- Who to Contact
- Times of the School Day.

Make sure your writing is neat so that people can read it easily.

> **Key terms**
>
> **layout** – the way a text is set out
> **headings** – words or phrases which break up the text and tell you what the next part is about; they are usually in large type

5 **Work as a class. Look at each other's work.**

1 Say what you think looks good.

2 What could be improved?

3 Is the handwriting clear and easy to read?

4 What have you learned so far about planning and writing an information leaflet?

Planning and writing a leaflet 2

This section will help you to:
- plan and write the rest of your leaflet
- choose and present information

1 Work as a class.

1 Talk about the things you can do in school outside lessons.
What activities and clubs are there at your school?
2 Talk about school rules. Which do new pupils need to know?

2 A student has started to write the back page of the Rushford High School leaflet. Look at what they have done so far. Read the labels. Then do the work opposite.

1 You can't tell readers everything about your school. You have to choose the most important information. Why has the writer chosen these activities?

2 Each activity and each rule has a bullet point. How does this help readers?

3 Which words are the headings?

Activities

Here are some of the things you can do and take part in here:

◇ _____   ◇ _____
◇ Reading Buddies   ◇ _____
◇ _____   ◇ Trips to _____
◇ Resource Centre   ◇ _____

School Rules

◇ Listen carefully to _____
◇ Make sure you _____
◇ Wear _____
◇ Walk _____

Lateness

If you are late, you need to _____
_____

Illness

If you are ill, please _____
_____

4 The activities are written in a list, not in sentences. Why do you think this is?

5 Rules often begin with imperatives, for example, *listen*, *wear*. Imperatives tell people what to do.

1. Make a list of activities that you can do at your school. Write them as bullet points.

2. List the most important rules in your school. Write them as bullet points. Use the sentence starters opposite to help you.

3 Work in pairs.

1. Take it in turns to talk to each other about what you should do if:

   a you can't come to school because you are ill

   b you are late.

2. Write up what you decide.

   • Use the headings **Lateness** and **Illness**.

   • Use the sentence starters opposite to help you.

4 Work on your own.

1. Write up your own back page using the material you have planned in this section.

2. Use the layout of the Rushford High School leaflet opposite to help you. Use the same headings:

   • Activities

   • School Rules

   • Lateness

   • Illness

3. Work hard to make it easy to read. It should look clear, neat and well spaced.

5 Work as a class. Look together at your leaflets.

1. Would each of them be suitable for parents and new pupils?

2. Which parts are particularly good in some leaflets?

3. How can you make an information text easy to read?

12 Explaining things carefully

This unit will help you to:
- give a spoken explanation
- discover the key features of explanation texts
- see how points are linked in paragraphs
- explain something using paragraphs

12.1 Asking questions and answering them

This section will help you to:
- ask questions to help you work out your ideas
- explain your answer clearly
- use a picture to help you explain

1 Work as a class. Make a list of words you can use to begin a question. For example:

Who? . . .

2 Work as a class.

1 Look at picture **A** opposite. Read the labels. They tell you how to work out what has happened.
2 What has been stolen? How do you know?

3 Work in pairs. Study the picture opposite. Take it in turns to ask and answer these questions. You may need to make up some information. Give reasons for your answers.

1 Why is the window broken?
2 Why was the drawer forced open?
3 Who left a muddy footprint and a screwdriver on the floor?
4 When did the robbery happen?
5 What happened to the thief's clothes?

WS **4** **Work in pairs. One of you is Mr Tait. The other is Robert.**

12.1

1 If you are Mr Tait:
Look at picture **B** opposite. Ask Robert *five* questions about the way he looks, and what he has been doing. For example:

2 If you are Robert:
Look at picture **C** opposite. It shows Robert's explanation. Work out an answer to each question you are asked. For example:

5 **Work as a class. Answer these questions.**

1 Study pictures **A** (page 115) and **B** (opposite). Mr Tait thinks Robert is the thief. Explain why he thinks this. Give as many reasons as you can.
2 Why is asking questions useful?
3 How did you show your ideas were sensible?
4 How did you use a picture to help explain something?

B Mr Tait asks Robert questions.

C This is Robert's explanation.

12.2

Reading an explanation text

This section will help you to:
- recognise some of the features of an explanation text
- find the main point in a paragraph
- work out what job the rest of the paragraph is doing

1 **Work as a class.**

1 The text opposite is an explanation. Find the title. Then answer these questions.

   a What is the text explaining?

   b What sorts of things do you think it will tell you?

2 Read the explanation opposite and look at the picture. Where does it answer these questions?

   a **What** is a lie detector?

   b **How** does it work?

   c **Why** is it useful?

   Most explanation texts answer these three main questions:
   Who? What? Why?

3 The text is divided into *paragraphs*. Share what you already know about paragraphs. For example:

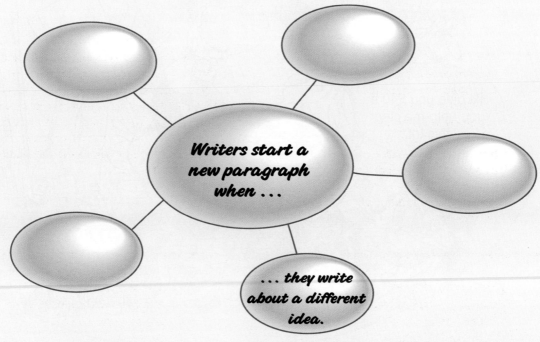

Writers start a new paragraph when . . .

. . . they write about a different idea.

How a Lie Detector Works

A A lie detector is a machine that notices how a person's body behaves while they are talking. When people tell the truth their bodies are calmer. However, once they start to lie their bodies behave differently. This is because they are stressed.

B The lie detector **is linked** to a set of machines. One machine **records** how fast a person **breathes**. Meanwhile another machine notes how fast their heart beats. At the same time a third machine measures how much they sweat.

C First **an interviewer** asks the person wearing the lie detector a question. Then **the person** says their answer. Meanwhile the interviewer is checking what the lie detector is showing. Sometimes **people** tell lies. However, the interviewer knows if an answer is a lie because the lie detector shows the person speaking is stressed.

1 A lie detector is used nowadays, so verb phrases are in the present tense.

2 These words show the text could be about anyone anywhere.

2 Work as a class. Find out how paragraphs are written.

1 Read this paragraph and its labels.

2 Explain the difference between main points and smaller points.

1 The **main point** shows you what the paragraph is about.

2 **Smaller points** give you more information.

3 **Link words** like these show how the points join together.

First an interviewer asks the person wearing the lie detector a question. Then the person says their answer. Meanwhile the interviewer is checking what the lie detector is showing. Sometimes people tell lies. However, the interviewer knows if an answer is a lie because the lie detector shows the person speaking is stressed.

3 Work in pairs. Do not look back at the last page.

1 The points below are from the same paragraph. They are mixed up. What order should they be in? Start with the main point.

A However, once they start to lie their bodies behave differently.

B This is because they are stressed.

C A lie detector is a machine that notices how a person's body behaves while they are talking.

D When people tell the truth their bodies are calmer.

2 Look at sentences **A** and **B**. List the link words.

4 **Work on your own. Read the paragraph below. Then do this work.**

1 Find and write out the main point.
2 Find and write out *one* smaller point.
3 Find and write out *one* link word.

> The lie detector is linked to a set of machines. One machine records how fast a person breathes. Meanwhile another machine notes how fast their heart beats. At the same time a third machine measures how much they sweat.

5 **Work as a class. How much can you remember about the way explanation texts are written? Test yourself with this quick quiz.**

1 Which *three* main questions do explanation texts answer?
2 Explanation texts are written in paragraphs. True or false?
3 What is the difference between smaller points and main points?
4 List *four* link words that may be used to join points together.
5 Complete this sentence:

> *Verb phrases in an explanation are often in the* ____ *tense.* This is because they often explain something that happens nowadays: *One machine records how fast a person breathes.*

12.3 Planning an explanation

> **This section will help you to:**
> - plan a series of points to explain something clearly
> - organise your points into paragraphs
> - work out the best order to put your paragraphs in

1 **Work as a class. Answer these questions.**

1 Which *two* sorts of points make up a paragraph?
2 What are the main features of an explanation?
  Complete the sentences in the box below.

> **Features of an explanation**
>
> An explanation text tells readers:
> - w_____ happens, for example: *Your body gets stressed when you tell a lie.*
> - w_____ it happens, for example: *Because it has to get ready to run or fight.*
> - h_____ it happens, for example: *Changes take place in your body.*
>
> An explanation text is:
> - often written in the _____ tense
> - organised by writing in p_____.

2 **Work as a class. This is how to plan a well organised explanation text. Read each step. Carry out each task.**

> **Step 1 Decide what you are explaining**
>
> Write down what you are going to explain. This will be your heading, for example: 'How a Lie Detector Works'.

Task 1 Study the illustration opposite. Write a sentence saying what it explains. This will be your heading.

A The person tells a lie.

It wasn't me!

B Brain – sends a message. It knows something is wrong. Chemicals make changes that tell the rest of the body to 'Get ready to run or fight!'

C Heart – beats faster. It pumps blood more strongly. Blood moves faster round the body.

D Lungs – breathe faster because more oxygen is needed.

E Hands – sweat. The liver is sending more energy to the heart and lungs so the blood heats up and the body gets hot.

> **Step 2** Choose your <u>main</u> points. Write them in a chart like the one below.

Task 2 Copy a chart like the one below. Then turn back to the illustration on page 123. Write the **main** points in column 2 of your chart.

1 Paragraph	2 Main points	3 Smaller points	4 Smaller points
Paragraph 1: introduction	• the person tells a lie	• truth will get them into trouble • don't want to get into trouble	• brain thinks of something to say – not the truth: 'it wasn't me!'
Paragraph 2	• the brain sends ...	• brain knows ...	
Paragraph 3	• the heart ...		
Paragraph 4	• the lungs ...		
Paragraph 5	• the hands ...		
Paragraph 6: conclusion	• a lot happens when you tell a lie ...		

> **Step 3** Decide what <u>smaller</u> points will go in each paragraph. Note them on your chart.

Task 3 Look back at page 123. Make a note of the smaller points you will make in each paragraph, in columns 3 and 4.

> **Step 4** Number your points in the order you will write about them.

Task 4 Number your points in your chart. Put them in the order you will write about them. Talk about why this is a good order for the points to go in.

3 Work as a class. Shut the book. Explain the *four* steps you need to follow when you plan an explanation text.

Linking points together

This section will help you to:
- write an explanation in paragraphs
- use different words to link points together

You may use the plan you made for the activity on page 124.

---

1 | **Work as a class.**

---

1 Share what you already know about:
- when to write a new paragraph
- the *kind of points* you make in a paragraph.

2 Now work on your own. The words in the box can link points together. Sort them into these three groups:

   a words you know and use

   b words you know but don't use

   c words you don't know – look up their meaning in a dictionary.

first	then	next	after	once	later
meanwhile	so	as	because	since	therefore

3 Work as a class. Look at the illustration on page 123. Complete the sentences below.

   a The person is in trouble **so** _____ .

   b The brain _____ **therefore** chemicals make changes.

   c _____ **then** the person starts to sweat.

   d **Since** the body is working harder it needs _____ .

I didn't do it!

2 Work as a class. You are going to use link words to join points in a paragraph. Read the example below. Then answer the question.

> **Step 1**
> Study your plan or the unfinished plan on page 124. Say each point as a sentence in your head. Which points should be joined together?
> For example:
> *The person tells a lie.   The truth will get them into trouble.*
>
> **Step 2**
> Choose the best link word to join those points. Check your new sentence makes sense before you write it down. For example:
> *The person tells a lie **because** the truth will get them into trouble.*

  1 How many ways can you link the following two points together?
- They don't want that to happen.
- Their brain thinks of something to say that is not true.

3 Work in pairs. Copy and complete the text below. Choose the best link word from the box to help you join the points.

first	then	next	after	once	later
meanwhile	so	as	because	since	therefore

The person tells a lie. _____ the brain sends a message to the rest of the body. It knows the lie might not be believed _____ the brain tells the body to get ready to run or fight.

_____ the heart receives the message and it starts to beat faster. _____ the blood can travel faster round the body. Blood is needed to carry food and oxygen to arms and legs _____ they need to get ready to run or fight.

4 **Work on your own. Choose either A or B.**

> **A** Use the plan you made for the activity on page 124. Write a paragraph about what happens to the liver.
>
> **B** Look below at label E which is taken from the illustration on page 123. Write a paragraph which links the points together.

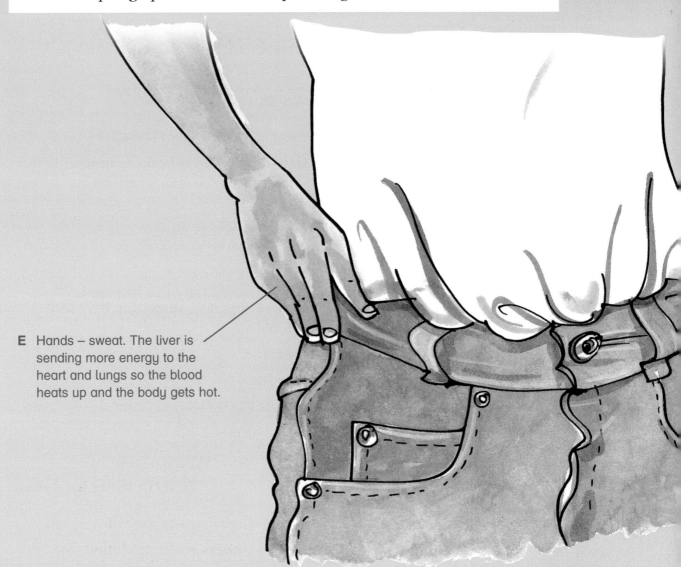

E Hands – sweat. The liver is sending more energy to the heart and lungs so the blood heats up and the body gets hot.

5 **Work in pairs. Read each other's work.**

> 1 Does it tell you what happens and why?
> 2 Spot the main point and one smaller point.
> 3 Underline the link words your partner used.
> 4 Tick each sentence that makes sense.

13 Giving instructions

13.1

This unit will help you to:
- give spoken instructions
- write instructions clearly
- use link words to order instructions

Giving spoken instructions

This section will help you to:
- give spoken instructions
- use time link words to order instructions

1 Work as a class. Which is a good instruction in the sentences below? Why?

- Show me your homework.
- Would you like to show me your homework?

2 Work as a class. Joseph is telling his Gran how to use the Internet. Read his instructions and the notes below. Then do this work.

1 Find as many imperative verbs as you can.
2 Find as many time link words as you can.
3 Why do we use time link words with instructions?

1 'Look' is an imperative or instruction word.

2 'First' is a time link word. Time link words show the order in which things happen.

3 In spoken instructions, we sometimes say, 'you' + verb.

Key term

imperatives – these are a type of verb we use for giving instructions. For example:
Listen! Open the door.

Instructions for Gran

Look, Granny, this is how to get onto the Internet. First, use the mouse to point the cursor at START. Then click.

Then, you point to PROGRAMS.

After that, find Internet Explorer in the list of programs.

Next, point the cursor and click on the words Internet Explorer and wait.

Now, type the website address in the box and click on GO. Success!

3 **Work in pairs. Put these instructions for using a mobile phone in the right order. For example, _1 = D._**

> **A** Then, you put in your PIN number.
>
> **B** Finally, wait for the person to answer.
>
> **C** Press the connect key.
>
> **D** First, you switch the mobile on.
>
> **E** After, key in the number of the person you want to call.

4 **Work on your own. Read these instructions for playing a computer game. Choose a time connective or imperative from the boxes below for each space.**

Time connectives	Imperatives
next, finally, then, after that	_look, click, place, start, point_

> First, use the mouse to point the cursor at START. Then click.
>
> Then, ___(a)___ the cursor at the word PROGRAMS.
>
> ___(b)___, you point at the word ACCESSORIES in the new menu.
>
> Now, ___(c)___ at the word GAMES. You will see a list of games.
>
> ___(d)___, point the cursor at the game you want to play and click the mouse.
>
> Now ___(e)___ playing.

5 **Read the remember box. Then tell your partner or the class how to do one of these:**

> • use a Gameboy
> • use a Playstation
> • walk from where you are to the main entrance
> • use a mobile phone.

> **Remember**
> When you give instructions, use:
> • imperatives, which tell someone what to do, for example: open, turn to, click on …
> • time link words to order the instructions, for example: first, then, next … .

Writing instructions

This section will help you to:
- write instructions clearly

1 Work as a class. Talk about where you see written instructions. What is important when you give instructions?

2 Work as a class. Read the instructions and notes below, then answer the questions.

> **1** What makes the order clear?
> **2** How else could you show this?

How to use a video
Instructions for a Martian or my Grandad!

1 Switch the power on.
2 Find the videotape you want to watch.
3 Put the videotape into the slot in the machine.
4 Press the play button on the remote control.
5 Relax and watch!

1 Each written instruction is an imperative.

2 Written instructions are simple and very clear.

3 Work in pairs. Match each instruction with the correct heading. The first one has been done for you.

Playing an electronic game

Headings	Instructions
1 Choose a game	**A** Now you're ready to play! Enjoy your game!
2 Choose a level	**B** Use the arrow key on the control panel to choose a game. Now press the GO button.
3 Check the rules of the game	**C** Choose a level of difficulty for the game. You can only play Level 1 at first – you'll have to win that one before you go to Level 2.
4 Have a go!	**D** Make sure you read the rules carefully. Press the GO button to play when you've finished reading.

4 Now work on your own. Write *three* instructions for playing a CD. Use the pictures to help you.

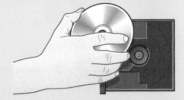

CLOSE
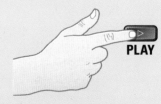
PLAY

5 Check your instructions. Answer these questions. Then show your instructions to someone else to check.

1 Did you use imperatives?

2 Did you use numbers or time link words to make the order clear?

3 Are your instructions clear and simple?

14 Offering advice

This unit will help you to:
- give spoken and written advice
- use role play to explore giving advice

14.1

Giving informal advice

This section will help you to:
- give informal advice, using role play

1 Work as a class. Talk about when someone gave you advice. What kinds of words did they use to make suggestions?

2 Work as a class. Alice wants to be a pop singer. Read what her friends said. Answer the questions.

1 Which suggestions sound like instructions? Why?
2 Which suggestions sound like friendly advice? Why?
3 What is the difference between instructions and advice?

I want to be a pop singer! What could I do to help me become one?

1 'You could' is a way of giving advice.

You could sing in the school concert. **A**

2 Imperatives (such as 'get') are often used to give advice.

Get a karaoke tape. **B**

Take singing lessons. **C**

Why don't you join a local band? **D**

3 'Why don't you' is a way of giving advice.

3 Work with a partner. Pete wants to be an actor. Talk about things he could do.

1 Choose the *two* best ideas.
2 Pretend your partner is Pete. Use 'advice words' to give him two pieces of friendly advice.

Things Pete could do: • act in the school play • take acting lessons • go to the theatre a lot • go to drama school • read lots of plays.	**Advice words:** • *You could …* • *Why don't you …* • *Have you thought about …* • *You might …* • *Maybe it would be good to …*

4 Work with a partner. Choose a situation to role play. Take it in turns to give advice.

Situations
- You want to go to the cinema but you are grounded.
- You are being bullied at school.
- You want a new hairstyle but you don't know which.
- You've upset your best friend.

For example:

Person A: I want to go to the cinema tonight but I'm grounded. What can I do?

Person B: Well, you could offer to wash up.

Person A: No, my mum still wouldn't let me.

Person B: Why don't you promise to keep your room tidy?

Remember to give advice in *two* different ways: friendly advice and strong advice. Think carefully about the advice words that you choose.

5 Work as a class. Listen to other people's role plays. Show them yours.

1 Tell them what you think of their advice.
2 How well did they use the different ways of giving advice?

Giving written advice 1

> **This section will help you to:**
> • write a leaflet that gives strong advice, using imperatives

1 **Work as a class. Talk about these questions.**

1 What is the Internet?
2 What is good about the Internet?
3 What do you have to be careful of?
4 What is an Internet chat room?

2 **Work as a class. Listen to your teacher read the leaflet below. Then answer these questions.**

1 Find *three* imperatives.
2 Why have imperatives been used?
3 What other ways can you give advice?
4 Why have they not been used here?

1 To instruct someone **not** to do something, use imperatives such as 'never' or 'don't'.

2 Imperatives are used to give strong advice.

Safe surfing for kids

1 Never tell anyone online your last name, address, phone number or where you go to school. And always keep passwords secret!

2 Tell your mum/dad or teacher if anything online makes you feel uncomfortable. (If they're not there, just sign off and tell them later.)

3 Never meet up with an online friend offline, unless your mum or dad goes with you. You can never be sure that people are telling the truth about themselves.

4 Make sure you know where files are from before you download them. They could have 'viruses' that damage your computer.

5 Don't send nasty messages or chain letters. If you get any, stop reading and tell your mum or dad.

3 **Work with a partner. You are going to design a leaflet giving strong advice to teenagers on how to stay safe when out at night.**

1 Brainstorm what you should do to stay safe when out at night. For example:

- *carry a mobile phone*

2 Write out at least *five* pieces of strong advice. Use these sentence starters to help you if you wish:

Always tell _____ .
Make sure _____ .
Don't _____ .
Never _____ .

4 **Work on your own. Design the leaflet about staying safe when out at night. Use the 'Safe surfing for kids' leaflet to help you.**

1 Think of a title for the leaflet.
2 Think about how you will lay out your leaflet.
3 Write out your strong pieces of advice. Number each piece of advice.

5 **Read your leaflet with a partner. Answer these questions.**

1 Is it good advice?
2 Does it make sense?
3 Have you used imperatives to give strong advice?
4 Have you used a full stop at the end of each sentence?

Giving written advice 2

This section will help you to:
- write a letter asking for advice
- write a letter giving advice

1 Work as a class. List ways in which you can give informal advice.

2 Work as a class. Read the letter to a problem page below. Then read Craig's reply. Answer these questions.

   1 List *three* different ways Craig gives advice.

   2 What kinds of punctuation does he use at the ends of sentences?

1 The letter begins with *what* the problem is, then explains *why* it's a problem.

Dear Craig,

I am 13 years old and I really want to be a pop star. It's all I've ever wanted to do. My parents think I am stupid. Do you think I am? They want me to be good at school. They say I should concentrate on my exams and forget my dreams. My friends say that I have a good voice. They think my voice is good enough to be famous. What should I do?

Yours,

Rio

2 The end of a sentence is always shown with punctuation.

3 The letter ends by asking for help.

Dear Rio,
Lots of teenagers want to be pop stars. I don't think you are stupid. Not many make it; in fact, very few become famous. Why don't you listen to your parents? They have a point. Try hard at school and get your exams. You may change your mind later and you will need qualifications. Why don't you join a local band? You could ask your friends to help you. You could also take singing lessons. This way, you will please your parents and become famous too.
Good luck!
Craig

3

14.1

Work in pairs. Read this letter. Decide if it needs a full stop or a question mark in each gap.

> Dear Marsha,
>
> I am twelve years old (1) I really want to be a model (2) I've tried to think of something else but I can't (3) I am good-looking and I like clothes (4) Am I old enough to become a model yet (5) I really don't know what to do (6) Can you help me (7)
>
> Thanks,
>
> Ally

4 **Work on your own.**

1 Write a letter asking for advice. Use Ally's letter and Rio's letter to help you. Choose one of these problems:
  - You want to be a DJ.
  - You want to be a footballer.
  - You have upset your brother or sister.

  Remember to:
  - begin by saying *what* the problem is
  - say *why* it's a problem
  - ask the person to help at the end
  - use full stops and question marks.

2 Swap letters with another student. Write an answer to the letter you are given. Remember to:
  - give advice in different ways:
    Why don't you ...?
    You could ...
    an imperative like *Tell ...* or *Don't ...*
  - use a full stop at the end of a sentence
  - use a question mark at the end of a question
  - check your work carefully.

5 **Share your letters as a class. Who has given the best advice? Why?**

15 Understanding the audience

This unit will help you to:
- understand how magazine covers attract their audience
- use a mind map to organise ideas
- write about a magazine

15.1 Understanding media and audience

This section will help you to:
- understand what 'media' means
- understand the media word 'audience'
- use a mind map to organise your ideas

1 Work as a class. What does the word 'audience' mean to you? Check the meaning in a dictionary. Finish this sentence in your own words:

The everyday meaning of the word 'audience' is . . .

2 Work as a class. Look at Tessa's mind map. It shows what twelve-year-old Tess likes to watch, listen to and read – the media she likes. Then answer the questions.

A mind map helps to organise your thoughts and ideas clearly.

1 Do you like the same things as Tess?

2 If Tess were 25 years old, what would change on the mind map?

3 If Tess were a boy, what might change on the mind map?

3 **Work in pairs.**

1 On your own, match one of the people below with the mind map:
   • Amrita, a 4-year-old girl   • Ben, a 15-year-old boy.
2 Explain your choice to your partner.
3 What other kind of media might each person like?

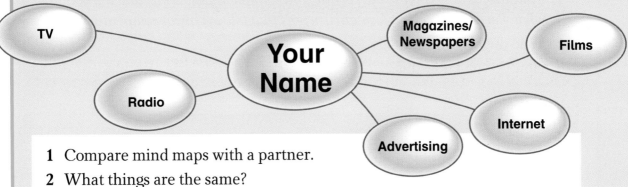

WS 4
15.1

Work on your own. Draw a mind map for the things you like reading, listening to and watching. Call it 'My Media'. Then do the tasks below.

1 Compare mind maps with a partner.
2 What things are the same?
3 What things are different?
4 Can you explain why some things are different or the same?

5 **As a class, finish these sentences together. Then learn the key terms.**

1 When we study the media, we look at …
2 What people like depends on …
3 The media reaches many audiences. The audience for *The Tweenies* is …
   The audience for *Which Motorbike* is …

Key terms

media – TV, magazines, newspapers, films, radio, music, the Internet, advertising
audience – the people reached by one of the media

Who is this magazine for?

This section will help you to:
- recognise the audience of a magazine from its cover

1 Work as a class. Read the two meanings of the word 'audience'. Which is the everyday meaning? Which meaning do we use when learning about the media?

A The group of people who a particular magazine, TV show or radio station is for.

B Anyone who sits and watches a TV programme, a concert or a play.

2 Work as a class. Read the key term below. Then look at the cover of *Mizz* opposite, and do this work.

1 Find these things on the cover: *title, price, main image, words that tell you what you can read about (contents), words that tell you about competitions.*

2 Who might buy this magazine?

3 How do you know this?

Key term

image – the word used for 'picture' when talking about the media

3 Work with a partner. Give reasons why each person below would or would not buy *Mizz*. Look at the cover for clues.

- Anna – girl, 13, likes playing sports
- Natasha – girl, 19, loves clubbing
- Neelam – girl, 12, loves free gifts
- Darren – boy, 13, loves football

4 Work in pairs. What can you say about the audience for *Mizz*? Note down your answers to these questions.

1 What sex is the audience for *Mizz*?

2 How old are they?

3 What is the audience of *Mizz* interested in?

4 What would grab their attention on this cover of *Mizz*?

5 Work as a class. Share your answers to activity 4. Then discuss these questions.

1 Who would buy *Mizz* magazine? Give reasons.
2 Who would not buy *Mizz* magazine? Give reasons.
3 What magazines do people in the class buy?
4 Why do they buy these magazines?

1 The way things look on the cover is very important.

2 Publishers want to make sure the magazine sells.

3 Publishers make the cover attractive to the 'right' audience, so they choose words, images and colours their audience likes.

15.3

Writing about a magazine cover

This section will help you to:
- say who the audience is from looking at a magazine cover
- write about how a magazine cover appeals to its audience

1 **Work as a class. Talk about these questions.**

1 Why are free gifts important on magazine covers?
2 What kind of free gift makes you buy a magazine?

2 **Work as a class.**

> **1** Look very closely at the magazine cover opposite. Then do this work.
>   **a** What is the title?
>   **b** List the images on the cover.
>   **c** What can you win in the competitions?
>   **d** Do the colour and style of the words look fun or serious?
>   **e** List the main colours on the cover.
> **2** Look at your answers to the questions again. Who do you think is the audience for this magazine? What age range might it appeal to (attract)?

3 **Work in pairs. Why does the cover of *Disney's Big Time* appeal to its audience? Copy and complete this chart.**

Feature from the magazine cover	Reasons why audience would like it
Title colours, style, and images	Look fun. More likely to appeal to boys.
Jimmy Neutron	Jimmy looks cool.
T.J. from *Recess*	
S Club 7	
Monsters from *Monsters, Inc.*	
Competition to win XBOX	
Competition to win trip to Disneyland	

4 **Work on your own. Write about the audience of *Disney's Big Time*. Begin like this:**

> The cover of the magazine is designed to appeal to . . .

5 **Work on your own. Explain why the cover appeals to the audience of the magazine. Use your chart from activity 3 to help you. Write sentences like this:**

> There is a competition to win an XBOX. Electronic games often appeal a lot to boys of this age.

Know your audience

This section will help you to:
- use what you know about audience
- use what you know about choosing words and images carefully

1 Work in pairs. You are ill in bed. Your friend wants to buy you a magazine. Tell them what to look for on the cover.

2 Work as a class. A publisher wants to publish a new magazine for boys aged 12 to 14. Look at the ideas for the cover, then answer the questions.

1 What will boys like about this cover?
2 What will grab their attention?
3 Explain what you think of the cover.
4 Would you buy it? Give reasons.

3 **Work in pairs.**

1 Decide which one of these article titles would grab the attention of teenage boys best. Explain why.
   A David Beckham talks tactics!
   B Football memories with Bobby Charlton
   C Win a skateboard!

4 **Work on your own. Design something to fill the gap on the cover opposite. Use the title of the article you chose in activity 3. Design it to grab the attention of teenage boys.**

1 Use the exact title of the article.
2 Choose a colour for the lettering.
3 Choose how you want to write the letters – the style.
4 Draw an image to go with the words (an outline will do).

5 **Share your design with a small group or the class.**

1 Describe your design.
2 Give *two* reasons why your design will make teenage boys buy the magazine.

Talking to the publisher

This section will help you to:
- prepare and give a talk about a magazine and its audience
- ask and answer questions about the talk

1 **Work as a class.**

1 Look again at the magazine design *Kool*. Copy out this chart with the headings:

Things that will appeal to teenage boys	Things that could be improved to appeal to teenage boys

2 Write each of these things under the heading you think is best:
- the title *Kool*
- the colour and style of lettering
- the main image of a boy on a skateboard
- the articles
- the review
- the competition.

2 **Work as a class. You are going to talk to the publishers of *Kool* magazine. They want to know if you think the magazine will appeal to teenage boys.**

1 Read the notes opposite.
2 What else do you think *will appeal* to teenage boys? Write notes in the same way. Use the same heading.

1 Bullet points make your notes clear and easy to speak from.

2 If you are giving a talk, it helps to have clear notes.

Notes for talk

Things that will appeal to teenage boys:	Reasons:
• Title	• Boys use the word 'Kool' for things they like. • They will think it's fun that it's spelt 'kool' not 'cool'

3 Work in pairs. Write notes for any things on the cover you think could be *improved to appeal* to teenage boys.

Things that will not appeal to teenage boys:	Reason:
• The competition for football gear •	• Many boys already have football kits. •

4 Work with a partner. Practise your talk to the publisher. Speak from your notes. Start off like this:

> I think the magazine *Kool* will/will not appeal to teenage boys. First of all, the title *Kool* will/will not appeal because …

Try to:

1 Speak in a clear voice that your partner can hear.
2 Use the connective 'because' before you give the reason.
3 End your talk by saying if you think the magazine will sell or not.
4 Listen to your partner's talk carefully.
5 Tell your partner one thing that will make their talk better.

5 Give your talk to the class. Speak in a loud, clear voice. After each talk, the class can:

• ask the speaker questions
• say *one* thing that was good about the talk
• say *one* thing that could be made better.

Persuading your audience

This unit will help you to:
- write an effective description
- understand how writers and presenters persuade people

Writing an effective description

> **This section will help you to:**
> - write an accurate description of a place
> - help readers imagine what it is really like
> - choose describing words carefully

1 **Work as a class.**

1 Read the words in the box. Sort them into two lists:
- names of things (nouns) such as *box*
- describing words (adjectives) such as *warm*.

dark	box	warm	cabin	carpet	fresh
lamp	curtain	drab	damp	door	cold
rain	bright	dull	dirty	cheerful	

2 Look at your list of adjectives. How can you sort them into two groups?

2 **Work as a class. Writers can tell readers facts and also give them a feeling for what a place is like. Read the description opposite. Answer the questions below.**

1 Read the last *three* highlighted descriptions. For each one say:
  a what is the fact
  b which word builds the feeling.
2 How has the writer made sure readers will not want to go on holiday there?

> **Remember** A **fact** is a piece of information that you can check is true. For example: *The cabin was in the woods.*

Cabin holiday

When we arrived at the cabin *it was drizzling.*
Each cabin was the colour of **cold** *mushroom soup.*
Ours also had a **dull** *green stain under the*
guttering. We stepped through the door onto the
5   **mud** *brown carpet.* The five of us filled the
cramped space. We looked around at the tired
white walls and drab pink curtains. There was
a smell of damp socks. This was our holiday home!

1   All the descriptions build
the same feeling.

2   The phrases in *italics* are all facts.

3   The describing words in **bold**
make you feel it was awful.

4   *Tired* and *white* are adjectives that
describe the noun, *walls.* Together,
the words make a noun phrase.
Tired white walls = a noun phrase.

3
16.1

**Work in pairs. Rewrite the description of the cabin. Make it seem a
cheerful place. Keep some of the facts. Change some of the adjectives.**

When we arrived at the cabin the sun was . . .

4
16.2

**Work on your own. Describe a place where you have stayed. Put in facts
and feelings. Show your reader what it was really like.**

1   Choose a room you have stayed in. It might be:
   • a place you lived in
   • somewhere you stayed on holiday
   • somewhere else.

2   Write down *five* facts about what it was like.

3   **a**   Decide how the place felt to you.
    b   Make a list of adjectives that will help you build that feeling.

4   Write your description. Give facts and use adjectives to give the feeling.

5

**Work as a class. Listen to each other's descriptions. Talk about these
questions.**

1   What is the main feeling of the place?
2   Which words help build that feeling?
3   Would you like to have stayed there or not? Why?

16.2

Persuading listeners

> **This section will help you to:**
> • find out how TV and radio presenters persuade listeners

> **Remember**
> • A **fact** is a piece of information you can check is true, for example:
>   *The hotel has two swimming pools.*
> • An **opinion** is somebody's point of view, for example:
>   *It was the worst week of my life!*

1 Work as a class. Read these sentences. Decide whether each one is a fact or an opinion.

> 1 There are 50 rooms in the hotel.
>
> 2 Grand Palace is by far the best hotel to stay in.
>
> 3 The swimming pool is always at 30 degrees.
>
> 4 Their triple chocolate ice-cream is fantastic!
>
> 5 You can even buy suntan lotion at reception.

2 Work as a class. Television and radio presenters want listeners to remember their opinions. Read this example. Then answer the questions.

> 1 What facts did you learn about Falton? Find at least *four*. Start with:
>   *There are donkeys at Falton.*
>
> 2 How does the presenter try to make you want to go there? Read the notes. Find at least *four* opinions. Start with: *Falton is such a friendly place …*

Falton

Falton is such a friendly place even the donkeys are smiling. The beaches are so beautiful… it's amazing here. Fantastic sunsets, gorgeous sand and wonderful swimming. It's heaven… and it's
5 only a ten-minute drive from town. After a hard day's sunbathing it is time to take in the night life. And San Antonio really buzzes at night. It's non-stop party time.

1 The presenter starts with humour.

2 The presenter is exaggerating here.

3 This verb and adjective (describing word) make it sound like a fun place.

3 Work in pairs. Read the speech bubbles below. Each presenter used method A, B or C to persuade listeners. Which presenter used which method?

A humour   **B** exaggeration   **C** words that touch listeners' feelings

1

> The Moroccan Mountain Trek weekend… is a once-in-a-lifetime challenge and a wonderful way to help a great charity. GO FOR IT!

2

> If you're going to bronze that body and you don't want to be lunch for 1,000 sand flies … buy one of the locally made beach mats. After all it can always double up as a chest-wig when you go out clubbing later.

3

> A smile, a cuddle and a bedtime story are such simple things, but they mean so much to these orphans. Could you give up a week of your summer holiday to work with the children in this African orphanage?

4 Work as a class. Look at the barge holiday below.

1 What are the *three* ways presenters can persuade listeners?
2 Use each of the three ways to persuade your listeners that this barge holiday is attractive.

16.3

Persuading readers

This section will help you to:
- find out how writers persuade different groups of readers
- understand why it matters how a text is set out

1 Work as a class.

1 Brainstorm lots of ideas to answer these questions.

   a How can *writers* try to persuade *readers* a place is great?

   b How can *presenters* try to persuade *listeners* a place is great?

2 Look at the advert opposite. It is trying to persuade people aged 18–30 to go on holiday to Benidorm. Say what each label should point to.

   A picture   **B** heading   **C** main text   **D** logo

Key term

appeal to – attract
For example: *Discos **appeal to** teenagers.*

2 Work as a class. The way the advert is set out appeals to the 'right' readers. Read the advert. Work out how it appeals to 18–30-year-olds.

1 Find:
- *two* facts 18–30-year-olds will like
- *one* opinion they will like
- exaggeration about something important to them
- a description that builds a feeling that will appeal to them.

2 Talk about the whole advert. List *six* things you should look for when you are reading an advertisement.

club 18-30

hotel nacional benidorm

bed & breakfast

official rating – 1 star

This hotel is so well situated you'll have everything at your fingertips. Pool here with free sunbeds for those serious sunbathing sessions. Small lounge next to reception and great bar that serves scrummy food with TV thrown in for good measure! Two sizzling beaches just down the road, or walk a little further to the old town where there are enough bars and eateries to have a massive night out. All rooms are simply furnished with private facilities and balcony. Sleep 1, 2–3 people.

1 *What is in the **brightest colour**? Why?*
Club 18–30 – The name of the holiday company persuades people between 18 and 30 that it is the right holiday for them.

2 *Why is this in the **biggest print and uses white and purple**?*
It's the name of the holiday place. It makes readers remember where they want to go.

3 *What takes **most space**? Why?*
Photographs show people enjoying the holiday. They persuade readers that they would enjoy it too.

Work in pairs. Read about Golden Sands holiday park below. Answer the questions.

1 What audience does the advert appeal to?

2 a What is given a lot of space? Why?

  b What is in bright colours? Why?

  c What is in large print or different colours? Why?

3 Where does the writer make the holiday sound great by using:

  a exaggeration   b five facts   c an opinion?

4 Explain to another pair how this advert persuades readers to go to Golden Sands.

GOLDEN SANDS
For a Fun Packed Family Holiday

A superb park in a beautiful location. There's something for everyone, from sandcastles to windsurfing. And there's so much to do – whether it's a round of golf or trying out water-skiing for the first time. There's a lively atmosphere after dark too... every night the entertainment is different. Feel all your cares disappear.

It's all on Park!
- Indoor and Outdoor Heated Pools
- Action! for 12–16+
- Playbarn
- Watersports Lake
- All-Weather Bowling Green
- Golf Course
- Moonlight Restaurant
- Chinese Takeaway
- 2 Mini-Markets
- Olly Octopus Kids' Club
- Sports Dome
- Professional Football Coaching
- Adventure Park
- Coarse Fishing Lake
- Munchies and Burgers
- Traditional Fish'n'Chips

Fantastic nights out... and a great family club room
- Fun Shows
- Live Bands, Cabaret and Music
- Choice of Bars

Out and About... Explore the Area
Thorpe Park   Windsor Castle   Legoland   Kempton Races
To Book Call 0500 7678   *or see your local travel agent*

This is the best holiday ever!

4 **Work on your own. Study the advertisement below. Answer the questions.**

1 What audience does the advert appeal to?
2 Pick *five* things the writer does to persuade this audience to choose this holiday.
3 Why do you think these things will work?

12

senior breaks at Blackpool for the

over 50s

Fun packed, full entertainment
Tribute to the late & great
Frank Sinatra, quizzes, gameshows,
live music, dancing, sing-alongs,
bingo, special acts,
the Blackpool Bluecoat Show

Quiet pint and a chat
Queen Victoria pub is a great place
to relax, unwind and
meet new friends

Sports and leisure
Snooker, darts, short mat bowls,
dance instruction, keep fit,
arts & crafts, heated indoor
swimming pool and aqua aerobics

Included in the price
is a trip to the famous
Tower Ballroom for an afternoon's
dancing with tea and scones.

Optional Extras
Coach trips to the Lake District,
Winter Gardens Show and
Pier Shows can be booked at
Pontin's Blackpool reception.

5 **Work as a class. What would you put in an advertisement to persuade students of your age to spend a weekend at a theme park?** *Think about: pictures, headings, use of colour, facts, opinions, descriptions and methods such as humour.*

17 Putting your point of view

This unit will help you to:
- back up your point of view when you talk
- work out how a writer developed main ideas
- persuade readers that your opinion is right

17.1 Backing up your point of view

This section will help you to:
- give your point of view
- back up your point of view

> **Key term**
>
> **point of view** – what one person thinks about something

1 Work as a class. Pick out the words in each sentence that show it is an opinion.

1 I think Alton Towers is the best theme park to go to.
2 In my opinion the most interesting place to visit is London Zoo.
3 In my view we should spend our day at a mountaineering centre.
4 I believe the Tower of London is an interesting place.
5 Going round a television studio would be great fun.

> **Remember**
> - A **fact** is a piece of information you can check is true, such as:
>   *There are lions at London Zoo.*
> - An **opinion** is somebody's point of view, for example:
>   *Ice skating is great fun.*

2 Work as a class. You are going to decide where to go on a class trip. Everyone must give an opinion and back it up. First, read the example below. Then answer this question.

1 In what order did the speaker talk about:

   A facts about the place

   B her own experience

   C her opinion about where to go

   D what the place would be like?

1 Give your opinion first.

Karting

In my opinion we should go to the Karting Race track at Send. I've been before and it was great fun. It's not too expensive **since** it only costs about £10 each for a session. It does not matter if you have not been karting before **because** they give everyone a driving lesson first. When I went someone checked you were properly strapped in and had on a crash helmet and pads before you could start driving so it is safe. You can just have fun driving as fast as you can round the course or you can have races. We could have our own Grand Prix.

2 Then make points that show why your opinion is right.

  a) You can use facts.

  b) You can give an example from your own experience.

  c) You can say what you think it would be like.

3 Use **connectives** such as **because** and **since** that link your points together.

WS **3**
17.1

Work in pairs. Where have you been that would make a good class outing? Persuade the rest of the class and your teacher that this is the best place to go on a trip. Make a note of your points in a chart like the one below.

1 Where, in your opinion should your class go?

2 Work out *three* reasons and how to back them up.

3 Use your notes to explain your opinion. Take it in turns to make points.

Opinion		
.... to go would be		
Three reasons why this is the best trip to go on	**Connectives you could use**	**Reasons backed up by**
1 *It is …*	*therefore* *so* *because* *since*	a fact:
2 *You can …*		an example from your own experience:
3 *There is/are …*		what it could be like:

4

Give your opinion to another pair. Listen to their opinion. Whose opinion is backed up most strongly? Why?

5

Work as a class.

1 Listen to each other's opinions. As you listen, decide:

• which points are backed up well

• how the speaker could have backed up their opinion more strongly.

2 After you have listened to everyone's opinion, vote on where your class would like to go.

How writers organise and support their points

This section will help you to:

- find the main points in a text
- see how each main point is developed
- understand how the whole text is put together
- explain how a writer puts across a point of view

1 **Work as a class. Sometimes a sentence can do more than one job. Read the sentences below.**

1 Which sentence:

  a gives an opinion

  b gives a fact

  c gives an example from the writer's own experience

  d says what a place might be like

  e is a question

  f is an exclamation?

> **A** I think the best theme park for our class to go to is Oakwood Park.
>
> **B** Some of the other theme parks I've been to were so busy you had to queue for over an hour to go on a ride.
>
> **C** If you have to spend a lot of time in queues then you can't go on so many rides, can you?
>
> **D** Then, when you do finally get on the ride, it's all over so quickly.
>
> **E** That is a total let-down!

Work as a class. Writers back up their opinions and try to persuade their readers they are right. Read how the writer does it in the first paragraph below. Then do the work opposite.

1 The paragraph begins with the main point. It is his **opinion**.

2 Then he makes smaller points to argue for his opinion:

  a) he uses facts

  b) he says what places could be like

  c) he tells you his opinion about other places.

3 Read the underlined sentences. The writer persuades you by using:

  a) a question you will agree with (known as a rhetorical question)

  b) an exclamation

  c) exaggeration.

Oakwood Park

I think the best theme park for our class to go to is Oakwood Park. Some of the other theme parks I've been to were so busy you had to queue for over an hour to go on a ride. <u>If you have to spend a lot of time in queues, then you can't go on so many rides, can you?</u> Then, when you do finally get on the ride, it's all over so quickly. <u>That is a total let-down</u>!

1 Now read the paragraph on this page. Which sentence should each of the labels **A–G** point to? (Remember, a sentence can do more than one job.)

Labels

> **A** The main point where he gives his main opinion.

These smaller points argue for his opinion.

> **B** He uses facts to give you useful information.

> **C** He says what the trip could be like.

> **D** He gives additional opinions.

The writer persuades you by using:

> **E** a question you will agree with

> **F** an exclamation to make you take special notice

> **G** exaggeration to help convince you.

[1] In my opinion Oakwood Park is very good value. [2] It is much cheaper than a lot of the other theme parks, probably because it is smaller. [3] It would not be too expensive, so everyone could come on the trip. [4] That's got to be good, hasn't it? [5] We could even get round all the rides in one day as it is smaller! It's the best theme park in the world!

WS 3
17.2

Work as a class. How has the writer backed up his opinion in the paragraph below?

> 1 Find at least one sentence where the writer:
>   a gives his main opinion
>   b uses facts to give you useful information
>   c says what The Bounce is like
>   d uses an exclamation to make you take special notice
>   e uses a question you will agree with
>   f uses exaggeration to help convince you.
>   Remember, a sentence can do more than one job!

The Bounce

By far the best ride at Oakwood is The Bounce. You have to pay extra to go on it (it was £30 when I went), but it's really worth it! It will take up to three people at a time so each group can split the cost between them. That's really good, isn't it? The Bounce is very popular because it is just like doing a bungee jump. You are lifted up very high and strapped into a special safety harness. Then one of you pulls a handle and you just DROP! The rope goes really tight and you swing for ages so it is really frightening! It's the most frightening thing in the world!

4 Work on your own. Write two paragraphs explaining how the writer argued that the best ride is The Bounce. Use the sentences below to help you.

Paragraph 1
The writer begins the paragraph with ...
He goes on to argue for his point of view by giving the reader facts such as ... which make you interested in the ride. He also gives further opinions that make the reader think it will be great fun, such as ...

Paragraph 2
The writer also persuades readers by using a ... such as, 'that's really good, isn't it?' and exclamations such as ... along with exaggeration such as ... to make readers take notice and convince you The Bounce really is the best ride.

5 Work as a class. Has the writer persuaded you that The Bounce could be the best ride? Give reasons for your answer.

Unit 17 ◆ Putting your point of view

Writing longer persuasive sentences

This section will help you to:
- write a longer sentence
- use a longer sentence to persuade

1 **Work as a class.**

1 Which of the sentences below:

   a makes only one point?

   b makes two points?

   c has most impact?

   d packs in most information?

> **A** The start of the ride, which is very high up, is great fun.
>
> **B** The rafts, which hold two people, are very safe.
>
> **C** First the raft is tipped up.
>
> **D** Then it is released.
>
> **E** Suddenly you are shooting along the water track, which is really exciting.

Explanation
Complex sentences

- Sentences **A**, **B** and **E** above, which made two points, were complex sentences.
- The writer has used complex sentences to:

  a) drop another point into a sentence:

    The rafts, <u>which hold two people</u>, are very safe.

  b) link their opinion to a fact:

    Suddenly you are shooting along the water track, which is really exciting.

                           fact   link word   opinion

Including more information, and linking an opinion to a fact in this way, can help persuade a reader.

2   Work as a class. Read the text below. It shows you one way to build this sort of complex sentence that can persuade a reader. Then answer the question.

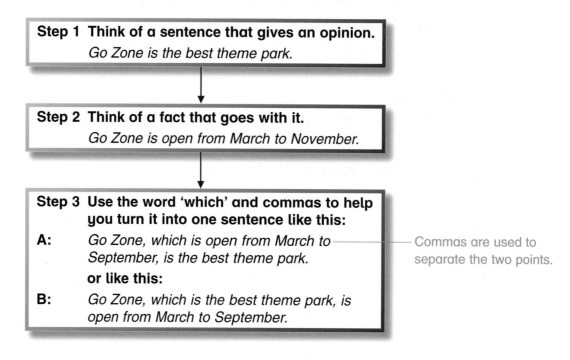

Step 1   **Think of a sentence that gives an opinion.**
Go Zone is the best theme park.

Step 2   **Think of a fact that goes with it.**
Go Zone is open from March to November.

Step 3   **Use the word 'which' and commas to help you turn it into one sentence like this:**
A: *Go Zone, which is open from March to September, is the best theme park.*
or like this:
B: *Go Zone, which is the best theme park, is open from March to September.*

Commas are used to separate the two points.

1   What do you read first about Go Zone in sentence A?
2   What do you read first about Go Zone in sentence B?
3   Which sentence (A or B) tells you the most persuasive thing about Go Zone first?
4   Read the fact and opinion below. Which is more persuasive – the fact or the opinion? Write a sentence using the word 'which' to link them. Put the most persuasive point first in the sentence so it will be noticed.

   • Go Zone closes at 6.30pm in summer.
   • Go Zone is great value!

 3   Work in pairs. Write *four* complex sentences that have 'which' in them.

17.3

1   Use the facts and opinions opposite.
2   Link a fact with an opinion in each sentence.
3   Put the parts of the sentences together in the order that you think works best. For example:

   Go Zone has over 50 different attractions and rides, which are great fun.

4   Choose one of your sentences. Explain why it is persuasive.

Facts

- Go Zone has over 50 different attractions and rides.
- It has 100 acres of gardens.
- You can hire a trundle cart for young children.
- There are eight places to eat.

Opinions

- The gardens are very beautiful.
- The attractions and rides are great fun.
- A trundle cart is very comfortable.
- The places to eat give lots of choice.

4   **Work on your own. Write a paragraph persuading people to go to Go Zone.**

1   Use some of the persuasive complex sentences you have put together in this unit.

2   Use some shorter sentences of your own that help persuade. A short sentence such as 'It's cool!' has lots of impact.

3   Begin like this:

> *For a great day out …*

5   **Work as a class. How could you rewrite the paragraph below to make it more persuasive?**

The safari park next door usually costs £10 per adult and £5.50 per child. The safari park next door is free to Go Zone visitors. The safari park has many rare animals in it. The safari park is famous throughout the world.

Putting your point of view

This section will help you to:
- write your opinion
- put your point of view
- persuade other people
- use different sorts of sentences

1 **Work as a class.**

1 Make up sentences about a theme park ride. Brainstorm sentences that:
   a give an opinion: *In my view ...*
   b give a fact
   c use exaggeration
   d are exclamations: *It is dreadful!*
2 Do any of your sentences do more than one job? For example, this sentence gives an opinion and uses an exclamation:
   In my view Nemesis is dreadful!

2 **As a class, read the questions below. They are written so readers will agree with the writer's point of view. Work out more questions like these about a theme park ride:**

A No one wants to fall out, do they?
   No one ... do they?
B Everyone wants to be scared, don't they?
   Everyone wants ... don't they?

 3 Work as a class. You are going to write your point of view about which theme park ride is best. You need to draft your point of view first. Follow the steps opposite.

4 **Work on your own. Write a best copy of your point of view. Make sure it makes sense.**

5 **Work as a class. Listen to each other's points of view. As you listen, try to spot one way the writer made their writing persuasive.**

How to write your point of view

Step 1   Decide which is the best theme park ride that you have been on. Write down your opinion. Write one sentence.

In my view the best theme park ride is Raging Water at Deerton Park.

Step 2   Work out different ways to back up your point of view:

- facts
- examples
- opinions.

a Write *three* sentences that give facts about your ride:

You travel at over 40 kph.

b Write *three* sentences saying what it is like. Give examples from your own experience:

I got soaked but I couldn't wait to go on it again.

c Write *three* sentences that give your opinion:

It was fantastic! It feels ...

Step 3   Work out how to make your writing persuasive.

Where can you use:

- exaggeration
- a question
- an exclamation
- a complex sentence
- a shorter sentence?

Improve sentences you have already written, or write some new ones.

a Write a sentence where you exaggerate how good the ride is. Use words in the box below or your own.

It is the most frightening ride in the universe.

| too | really | extremely | most | total | very |

b Write one complex sentence with a fact and an opinion in it.

The bends and drops, which include a loop-the-loop, are fantastic.

c Write a question, like the ones you did earlier, which readers will agree with:

Everyone loves getting soaked, don't they?

d Write a sentence that is an exclamation. You can use it to end your writing:

You won't find better!

18 Presenting a balanced argument

18.1

This unit will help you to:
- say and write what you think
- listen to and write about what other people think

Different points of view

This section will help you to:
- understand different points of view
- give your views about school uniform

1 Work as a class. Read this sentence. How do you know it is someone's point of view?

I think school uniform is a great idea.

2 Work as a class. Read this extract from an article about school uniform, and the notes. Then answer the questions.

1 There are two points of view about uniform. What are they?
2 Do you know who the writer agrees with?
3 Who do you agree with?

1 This tells us it is one person's point of view.

2 The writer tells us why Fraser does not like school uniform.

3 These words tell us that Mrs Ahmed does not agree with Fraser.

4 This tells us it is one person's point of view.

Is it thumbs down to school uniform?

Fraser hates wearing school uniform. He thinks it's very expensive. Fraser complained that his shoes cost £50. He says, 'I could buy a great pair of trainers for that.' Mrs Ahmed, his head teacher, thinks the opposite.
5 She thinks students look smart in uniform. 'They would look really messy in their own clothes,' she stated.

3 **Work in pairs.**

1 Read these points about school uniform. Discuss each point.

   A School uniform is bad because it's ugly.

   B Everyone looks smart in uniform.

   C Uniform is very expensive.

   D Everyone looks better in their own clothes.

   E Students get bullied if their clothes are different.

   F School is for learning, not fashion.

2 Has your discussion changed your mind at all? If so, how?

4 **Work in pairs.**

1 A 'video box' shows someone giving their point of view on video.
   Read below what Mrs Ahmed, the head teacher, said in the video box.

2 Take it in turns to imagine you are on the video box. Tell your partner
   what you think about school uniform. Talk about the points in activity **3**.
   Use phrases like:

   • *In my opinion ...*   • *I know ... but ...*   • *I think ...*

I really like school uniform. In my opinion, school is for learning, not for fashion. I know students don't like it, but they need to think about their lessons rather than what their friends are wearing. I think students could get bullied if their clothes are different. If everyone looks the same, this doesn't happen.

5 **Work as a class.**

1 Give your video box talk to the class or the camera.

2 Did anybody change their mind about school uniform because of what
   someone said? If so, talk about why.

Finding out what people think

> **This section will help you to:**
> • use a survey to support points of view
> • talk and write about what the survey shows

1 Work as a class. Finish this sentence:

A survey is when you ask questions to...

2 As a class, read the school uniform survey done by class 7A. Then answer the questions.

   1 How many students:
     a like school uniform
     b don't like school uniform
     c prefer trainers to shoes
     d think school would be like a fashion show if students chose what to wear
     e think students wouldn't get bullied if they chose what to wear?
   2 A few students like school uniform. True or false?

School uniform survey		
Questions	Yes	No
Do you like school uniform?	2	8
Do you prefer trainers to shoes?	8	2
Would school be like a fashion show if students chose what to wear?	3	7
Would students get bullied if they chose what to wear?	6	4

— **Most** students don't like school uniform.

3 Now work in pairs. Use the information in the chart in activity 2 to complete the sentences below. Use the words 'most' and 'a few'.

1 _____ students don't think school would be like a fashion show if students chose what to wear.

2 _____ students think school would be like a fashion show if students chose what to wear.

3 _____ students don't think students would get bullied if they chose what to wear.

4 _____ students think students would get bullied if they chose what to wear.

4 Work as a class to carry out the same survey. Each student must answer all the questions.

Put a tick for each student in the correct column. Add up the ticks at the end like this:

Questions	Yes	No
Do you like school uniform?	✓✓✓✓✓✓✓✓ = 8	✓✓ = 2

5 Work on your own. Write sentences using 'most' and 'a few' to explain the information in your survey, for example:

Most students in the class like school uniform.

Writing what you think

This section will help you to:
- write what you think about school uniform
- use your survey results in your writing

1 Work as a class. Write down *four* true sentences about class 7A's survey on page 170. Put together a 'head' and a 'tail' from the chart below, for example:

Students usually don't like school uniform.

Heads	Tails
A few students …	… don't like school uniform.
	… prefer trainers to shoes.
	… think school would be a fashion show if students chose what to wear.
Students usually …	… think that students would get bullied if they chose what to wear.

2 Work as a class. Read this paragraph written by Joe in class 7A. Read the labels, then answer the questions.

  1 What is the paragraph about?

  2 Which sentence tells us what 7A think?

  3 Which sentence tells us what Joe thinks?

Students usually don't like school uniform. In my survey, most students didn't like school uniform but a few did. I don't like school uniform because I don't feel comfortable and I don't like the colour. I would prefer to wear my own clothes.

1 This sentence is the topic sentence. It tells you the main thing the paragraph is about.

2 The connective **because** links *what* he thinks with *why* he thinks it.

3 Now work on your own. Write a paragraph like Joe's. Use your class survey and your own opinion about school uniform. Use the writing frame to help you. Check your work with a partner.

Students usually _____ (*like/don't like*) school uniform. In my survey, most students _____ but a few _____.
I _____ (*like/don't like*) school uniform because _____
_____
_____.

4 Work on your own to write the next paragraph. Use the writing frame to help you.

Students usually _____ (*like/don't like*) trainers. In my survey,
_____ .
I _____ trainers
because _____ .

5 Work on your own. Write *two* more paragraphs about school uniform to follow on from activities 3 and 4. Use the same pattern as before. Use these topic sentences to start each paragraph.

Paragraph 3: Students usually (*think/don't think*) school would be a fashion show if students didn't wear uniform.

Paragraph 4: Students usually (*think/don't think*) that students would get bullied if they didn't wear uniform.

Presenting an argument

This section will help you to:
- write an introduction
- write a conclusion

1 Work as a class. Talk about why it is important to listen to other people's opinions.

2 Work as a class. Read this article. You have seen part of it before. Then answer the questions.

   1 What does an introduction tell the reader?

   2 What is the job of a conclusion?

   3 What does this conclusion include?

Is it thumbs down to school uniform?

1 An **introduction** is a paragraph that begins a piece of writing.

Last Friday was National Non-Uniform Day. Students everywhere chose what they wanted to wear to school. But what do pupils and teachers really think about school uniform?

Fraser hates wearing school uniform. He thinks it's very expensive. Fraser complained that his shoes cost £50. He says, 'I could buy a great pair of trainers for that.'

Mrs Ahmed, his head teacher, thinks the opposite. She thinks students look smart in uniform. 'They would look really messy in their own clothes,' she stated.

2 A **conclusion** is a paragraph that ends a piece of writing.

Teachers and students will always discuss school uniform. As a parent, I think school uniform is a good idea. I don't want to argue with my children every morning about what they can or cannot wear to school.

5

10

3 Work on your own. You have already written four paragraphs for section 18.3. They will be the middle of your own piece called, 'Is it thumbs down to school uniform?' Now write the introduction.

> **1** First, read your paragraphs again.
>
> **2** Copy and finish these sentences. This paragraph will be your introduction.
>
> > I am writing about _____.
> >
> > School uniform is a good subject to write about because _____
> >
> > _____.
> >
> > I did a survey to find out _____
> >
> > _____.

4 Work with a partner.

> **1** Take it in turns to talk about your final ideas about school uniform.
>
> **2** On your own, write your conclusion. Begin like this:
>
> > Teachers and students will always discuss school uniform.
> > In my opinion, ...
>
> **3** Read your introduction and conclusion to your partner.
> Do they make sense?

5 Work on your own. Now write your paragraphs in a sensible order in your best handwriting.

> **1** Include:
> - the title: 'Is it thumbs down to school uniform?'
> - your introduction
> - your four middle paragraphs
> - your conclusion.
>
> **2** Check your work. Have you used full stops and capital letters?
>
> **3** Share your work with the class. Ask the class to tell you *two* good points about your piece of writing.

19 Spelling strategies

This unit will help you to:
- learn to spell tricky words
- choose the best strategy to help you

This will help you spell words such as: beautiful, conclusion, definite, remember, Saturday

Most people find some words hard to spell. You already know lots about spelling. Even when you make a mistake, some letters are right:

✓✓✓
becos   because

When you don't know how to spell a word:
- have a try
- check it looks right
- check in the dictionary.

The six strategies in this unit will help you **learn** to spell tricky words.

Key term

spelling strategy – a way to remember how to spell a tricky word

---

1 **Read about breaking words into syllables to remember how to spell them.**

Strategy 1: Break the word into syllables

Step 1 Say the word and count the syllables: *re-mem-ber*.
                                                       1   2   3

Step 2 Write the word. Draw a line between each syllable: *re / mem / ber*.

Step 3 Make sure you can spell each syllable.

Step 4 Say and write the whole word.
            Check it – does it look right?
            Check with a dictionary if you are not sure.

remember

---

2 **Use Strategy 1.**

1 Learn to spell: *performance*, *landscape*.
2 Choose *two* words you find it difficult to spell. Use this strategy to learn them.

---

3 **Read about sounding words out to spell them correctly.**

Strategy 2: Sound the word out

Step 1 Say the word slowly and count the sounds: *d r u m*.
                                                       1 2 3 4

Step 2 Say the word slowly and write each sound – check it.

Step 3 Say and write the whole word. Check it – does it look right?
            Check with a dictionary if you are not sure.

4 Use Strategy 2.

> **1** Learn to spell: *atlas, inhabit*.
>
> **2** Choose *two* words you find it difficult to spell. Use this strategy to learn them.

5 Read about finding and remembering the tricky part of a word.

> **Strategy 3: Find and remember the tricky part**
>
> **Step 1** Look carefully at the word: *because*.
>
> **Step 2** Underline the tricky part: *bec<u>au</u>se*.
>
> **Step 3** You know the rest, so learn the tricky part: *a-u-s-e (because)*.
>
> **Step 4** Say and write the whole word.
> Check it – does it look right?
> Check with a dictionary if you are not sure.

because

6 Use Strategy 3.

> **1** Learn to spell: *beautiful, column*.
>
> **2** Choose *two* words you find it difficult to spell. Use this strategy to learn them.

7 Read about using words you know to spell, to help you.

> **Strategy 4: Find another word that sounds similar**
>
> **Step 1** Say the word: *flight*. Find another word that sounds similar.
> Hint: try rhyme.
>
> **Step 2** Write down the word that sounds similar: *light*.
>
> **Step 3** Add or change letters until it looks like the word you want to spell:
> *f - light*.
>
> **Step 4** Say and write the whole word.
> Check it – does it look right?
> Check with a dictionary if you are not sure.

flight

8 Use Strategy 4.

> **1** Learn to spell: *wealth, imagery*.
>
> **2** Choose *two* words you find it difficult to spell. Use this strategy to learn them.

9 **Read about catchy ways to remember spellings.**

> **Strategy 5: Think of a catchy way to remember the spelling**
>
> **Step 1** Look at the word. Think of a catchy way to remember the spelling. This is called a **mnemonic**. You can use this strategy to remember just the tricky part of a word, too. For example:

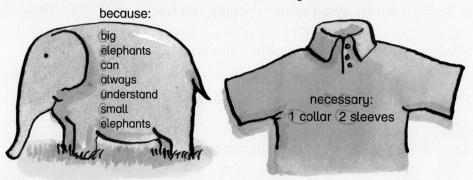

because:
big
elephants
can
always
understand
small
elephants

necessary:
1 collar 2 sleeves

> **Step 2** Practise the catchy phrase a few times. Write the word as you say it.
>
> **Step 3** Say and write the whole word using the catchy phrase.
> Check it – does it look right?
> Check with a dictionary if you are not sure.

10 **Use Strategy 5.**

1 Learn to spell: *parallel, communication*.

2 Choose *two* words you find it difficult to spell. Use this strategy to learn them.

11 **Read about five steps to help you remember a spelling.**

> **Strategy 6: Look, Say, Cover, Write, Check**
>
> | 1 Look | 2 Say | 3 Cover | 4 Write | 5 Check |
> |---|---|---|---|---|
> | | | | | |
>
> **Step 1** Look carefully at the word.
>
> **Step 2** Say the word and all the letters in order.
>
> forty
> f-o-r-t-y
>
> **Step 3** Cover the word. Say the word and the letters in order.
>
> **Step 4** Write the word as you say the word and the letters.
>
> **Step 5** Check the word – did you get it right? If not, start again.

12 **Use Strategy 6.**

1 Learn to spell: *although, tomorrow*.

2 Choose *two* words you find it difficult to spell. Use this strategy to learn them.

High-frequency words

This unit will help you to:
• learn to spell words you use often
This will help you to spell words such as:
where, there, here; should, could, would;
which, why, when

g. page 5:
here, when,
hy

Some words are used more often when you write. These are called **high-frequency words**. Writing is easier when you can spell them.

1 **Use strategy 4 (page 177).** Look at these words.

> **1** *where   there   here*
>
> **2** Write out the part that is the same in each word.
>
> **3** Learn to spell the part that is the same (Strategy 4). You have nearly learned all three words!

2 **Use strategy 6 (page 178).** Look at each group of words below.

> **1** *should, could, would   which, why, when*
>
> **2** Write out the part that is the same.
>
> **3** Use Look, Say, Cover, Write, Check to learn these words (Strategy 6).

3 **Work out the best strategy to use for different words.** Read the words in the box. Look carefully at the groups of letters in each word.

> **1**
>
> | near, word, hear, light, poster, sight, tight, paper, sister, night, clear, water, world, work, fear, worth |
> | --- |
>
> **2** Sort these words into *four* groups.
>
> **3** Learn each group using the strategy that would work best from Unit 19.

4 **Look at your own writing.**

> **1** Find *three* high-frequency words you often get wrong.
>
> **2** Learn each one using the strategy that would work best from Unit 19.
>
> **3** Remember to spell them right next time you use them!

CVC words

This unit will help you to:
- read and write words with the pattern consonant – vowel – consonant

This will help you to spell words such as: hot, tap

e.g. page 17:
day, car, not

The **vowels** are in **bold**. All the other letters are **consonants**:

a b c d **e** f g h **i** j k l m n **o** p q r s t **u** v w x y z

Lots of words have a consonant – vowel – consonant pattern (CVC), for example:

less   bit   hot   cut   map   plot

1 **Make your own CVC words.**

1 Work on your own. Write these letters on squares of paper.

a   e   i   o   u   t   n   s   h   p

2 Make as many CVC words as you can.
3 Write them down.
4 Work with a partner to compare your lists.

2 **Work on your own.**

1 Complete these words by adding vowels:

l_ss   s_ng   b_st   cl_ck

2 Can you make different words by changing the vowels?

3 How many words can you make?

22 Long 'A'

g. page 28:
fraid, away,
ay

This unit will help you to:
- hear the long 'A' sound in words
- know its most common spellings

This will help you to spell words such as: celebrate, aim

Say these words aloud:

celebrate   *aim*

The underlined parts sound like the name of the letter 'A'. This is called 'long A'. There are several ways to spell long 'A'.

1 Learn to recognize words with long the 'A' sound.

Read this text aloud. Find *ten* words with the long 'A' sound.
Remember: listen for the long 'A' sound. Don't just look for the letter 'a'.

> **Art lesson**
>
> Today you are going to frame a picture of your friend's face. First, spray-paint the card. Make a space and lay the card flat. Wait for it to dry. Then place a portrait of your friend in the middle.

2 Find *three* main ways to spell the long 'A' sound.

1 Write down the ten long 'A' words from 'Art lesson'.
2 Sort them into *three* groups. Write them in columns like this:

-ay	a-e	ai
today	*frame*	*paint*

3 Choose *three* words with the long 'A' sound that you find it difficult to spell. For example: clay, blame, afraid. Learn the words using the strategy that would work best from Unit 19.

23 Long 'I'

This unit will help you to:
- hear the long 'I' sound
- know its most common spellings

This will help you to spell words such as: life, lighting, climb

e.g. page 31: silence, line

Say these words aloud:

life   lighting   climb

The underlined parts sound like the name of the letter 'I'.
This is called 'long I'. There are several ways to spell long 'I'.

1 **Learn to recognize words with the long 'I' sound.**

Read this text aloud. Find *twelve* words with the long 'I' sound.

Remember: listen for the long 'I' sound. Don't just look for the letter 'i'.

> ## Tonight at Nine
> Now it is time for the sporting highlights.
>
> The 200-metre champion, Miles, crossed the line just behind Smith.
>
> Later he said, 'My time was fine. It was tight. I thought I would die if I tried harder.'

2 **Find *three* main ways to spell the long 'I' sound.**

1 Write down the long 'I' words from 'Tonight at Nine'.
2 Sort them into *four* groups. Write them in columns like this:

i-e	igh	i	other
nine	tonight	behind	die
			my

3 **Choose *three* words with the long 'I' sound that you find it difficult to spell. For example: bite, sigh, remind, lie, type. Learn the words using the strategy that would work best from Unit 19.**

Prefixes

.g. page 68:
ntidy

This unit will help you to:
- understand how prefixes change the meanings of words
- learn the spelling rule for adding a prefix

This will help you to spell words such as:
disappear, uncertain, impatient

Some words are built up from smaller words and parts of words. For example:

dis/appear

prefix   **root word**

1 **Think about how the prefix 'dis' works.**

1 How does the prefix 'dis' change the meaning of the word 'appear'?

2 Does 'dis' change these words in the same way?

dis/appoint   **dis**/approve   **dis**/respect

2 **Join each prefix below to a word, to make another word.**

un-   im-   possible   kind

mis-   non-   sense   lead

3 **Read this text aloud. Find *seven* words with prefixes. Write them out like this: non/sense.**

A local club has been accused of playing music too loud. The owner said, 'It is nonsense to say that the music is too loud. The matter has been misreported. Our neighbours dislike the club and are misleading the public. It is unkind and unfair. It is impossible to attract young people with quiet music!'

4 **Use a dictionary.**

1 Find *five* other words with the prefixes 'mis', 'dis' or 'un'.

2 Does the prefix always turn the word into its opposite?

3 Use a strategy from Unit 19 to learn *three* of the words that you have difficulty spelling.

Spelling rule: When you add a prefix to a root word the spelling stays the same, for example: ***appear*** ⟶ ***dis/appear***

25 Suffixes: verb endings

e.g. page 25: snatched, holding

This unit will help you to:
- learn spelling rules for adding suffixes '-ing' and '-ed' to a verb

This will help you to spell words such as: snatch – snatched, horrify – horrified, pop – popped, smile – smiling

Verbs tell us what is happening: *talk*, *grab*.
Verb endings change to show:
- who is doing the action (*person*)
- when it is happening (*tense*).

talk	talks	talking	talked
root word		**suffix**	

1 **Read this text from Unit 3. Then find and write down *ten* verbs with the suffixes '-ing', or '-ed'.**

I leapt across the room and snatched the frog Darryn Peck was holding and squeezed his cheeks hard so his red lips popped open and stuffed the frog into his mouth and grabbed the sticky tape from the art table and wound it round and round his head till there was none left. The others all stared at me, mouths open, horrified. Then they quickly closed their mouths. It was almost amusing.

Spelling rules:
- Most verbs just add the suffix to the root word: *jump* ——→ *jumped*, *enjoy* ——→ *enjoying*.
- In some verbs, the root word changes when you add the suffix.

Rule A: Verbs ending with a vowel and a consonant	Double the last consonant and add the suffix: *pop* ——→ *popped*
Rule B: Verbs ending with a consonant and 'y'	**1** Change 'y' to 'i' and add '-ed': *horrify* ——→ *horrified* **2** Leave the 'y' and add '-ing': *horrify* ——→ *horrifying*
Rule C: Verbs ending with an 'e'	Drop the last 'e' and add the suffix: *smile* ——→ *smiling*
Rule D: Other verbs	Add the suffix: *jump* ——→ *jumped*

2 **Read the rules above. Look at your list of words. Decide which rule each word follows. Write *four* lists: A, B, C and D.**

Plurals

g. page 23:
irds,
andwiches

> **This unit will help you to:**
> • learn the spelling rules for making nouns plural (more than one)
>
> *This will help you to spell plurals of words such as:*
> country → countries   church → churches   liquid → liquids

A *singular* noun means just one of something, for example: *one trainer*.

A *plural* noun means more than one, for example: *a pair of trainers*.

Most nouns change their spelling when they are plural, for example:

body ——→ bodies   prefix ——→ prefixes   citizen ——→ citizens

1 **Read the notice. Find and write down *five* plural nouns. Write the singular noun beside each one.**

rehearsals – rehearsal

Play rehearsals

The play rehearsals will be on Mondays after school. Students wishing to take part must return their reply slips to one of the drama teachers by this Friday. The list of actors will be posted on the drama room door on Monday morning.

Spelling rules:

Rule A: Nouns ending with 'sh', 's', 'x', 'z' or 'ch'	Add 'es' to make it easier to say: atlas——▶atlases church——▶churches
Rule B: Nouns ending in a consonant and 'y'	Change the 'y' to 'ie' and add 's': country——▶countries
Rule C: Most other nouns	Just add 's': liquid——▶liquids
Rule D: Some words don't follow any of these rules	Examples include: knife – knives; wife – wives; life – lives; tomato – tomatoes; potato –potatoes; sheep – sheep

2 **When Robert wrote his shopping list he forgot how to make nouns into plurals. Copy out his list using plural nouns. Then read the rules above. Decide which rules each word follows. Write *four* lists: A, B, C, D.**

Shopping list for Amy and John's two party

3 box of juice   6 knife   3 prize
4 large packet of crisp   2 large dish   12 candle
6 sandwich   2 bag of party popper

Apostrophes – missing letters

This unit will help you to:
- use an apostrophe to write a contraction

This will help you to spell words such as:
they'll (they will); you're (you are);
haven't (have not)

**e.g. page 23:
I'm, I'd, I've**

An apostrophe shows that a letter is missing when two words are made into one: I am ⟶ I'm   you have ⟶ you've

Shortened words are called **contractions**. We use contractions when we talk and in informal writing.

1   **Read these texts.**

1 Which one is written and which one is spoken?
2 How can you tell?

A
> You have won £1000. We will post a cheque to you.

B
> You've won £1000. We'll post a cheque to you.

2   **Change these formal texts into informal texts. Write them out, turning the underlined words into contractions.**

A   I <u>cannot</u> be there until 6pm. <u>Do not</u> wait.

B   <u>You are</u> correct. <u>I have</u> another question.

C   <u>They will</u> show you the way. I <u>have not</u> got a map.

D   <u>We are</u> in class N. <u>She is</u> our teacher.

3   **Choose *three* of these words to learn. Use the strategy that works best from Unit 19.**

> haven't, you've, can't, don't, we'll, she's, you're, they're

28 Subject words

This unit will help you to:
• learn to spell key words for different subjects
• choose the most useful strategy for learning these words
This will help you to spell words such as: colour, display, decimal, measure, poetry

In every subject there are some words you often need to read and write. These are **key words**. Learn to spell them!

Remember: different strategies help you to learn different types of words.

Strategy (see Unit 19)	Example
1 Does it break up easily into syllables?	dis/play
2 Does it help to sound the word out?	inhabit
3 Can you spell most of it? Learn the hard part.	decimal (soft 'c', not 's')

1 **Join the syllables to make words:**

es   ti   mate   pro   duc   tion

2 **Sound out the words below as you spell them.**

satisfy   media   poetry   history

3 **Write out these words. Underline the hard part.**

chemical   science   system

4 **Look at the words in the table.**

1 Choose *five* that will be useful to you.

2 Choose the strategy that would work best from Unit 19 for each one and learn to spell it.

Maths	English	Geography	Science	D & T
decimal	rhyme	abroad	absorb	brief
estimate	scene	country	chemical	design
measure	simile	poverty	cycle	evaluation

5 **Look at some writing you have done in another subject.**

1 Choose *three* key words you find hard to spell.

2 Choose a strategy for each word and learn to spell it.

29 Using a dictionary

This unit will help you to:

• use a dictionary to check words you are not sure how to spell

This will help you to spell words from different subjects such as: charcoal, evaluation, simile, international, weather

---

Dictionaries tell you:

• how to spell words
• what words mean
• how to pronounce words.

Words in dictionaries are listed in alphabetical order.

1 **Write out the following words in alphabetical order.**

| sharp | long | thin | wet | bumpy | curly | hot |

2 **Read about the dictionary quartiles, below. Say which quartile each of these words is in.**

weather   international   charcoal   simile   evaluation

Think about the dictionary in four quarters. These are called **quartiles**.

a b c d e f g **h i j k l m** *n o p q r s* **t u v w x y z**

1   2   3   4

When you look up a word, go straight to the quartile you need. This is the quickest way to use a dictionary.

3   **Read about how to find the word you need in a dictionary.**

Follow these steps to look up a word you are not sure how to spell, for example, *investigate*:

Step 1   Say the word and write down the letters you can hear:
i – vs – t – gate.

Step 2   Say it again. Check you have the first two or three letters:
invs – t – gate.

Step 3   Look at the first letter (*i*). Find the correct quartile of the dictionary.

Step 4   Look at the second letter (*n*). *Investigate* will be in the second half of the 'i' words.

Step 5   Look at the third letter (*v*). *Investigate* will be near the end of the words beginning with 'in'.

4   **Find the word 'investigate' on this dictionary page.**

idle
ill
impossible
investigate
itch
ivy

5   **Work in pairs. Have a dictionary race to find these words:**

charcoal   evaluation   simile   international   weather

6   **Work in pairs.**

1   Person A chooses a word from the dictionary and reads it aloud.
2   Person B follows the five steps above to look it up. How long did it take?
3   Now swap over.

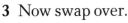

7   **Work on your own.**

1   Find *three* words that you have spelled wrongly in your own writing.
2   Follow the five steps above to look them up in the dictionary.

30 Checking your own work

This unit will help you to:
- notice which words you often spell wrongly in your own writing
- learn to spell them so that writing becomes easier and quicker

When you can spell well:

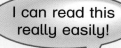

This is easy!

I can read this really easily!

This is good!

Writing is easier and quicker.

Your writing is easier for other people to read.

People stop moaning about your spelling. They enjoy what you have written.

It is hard to spot mistakes in your own writing. Follow the tips below.

1 **Read Tip 1.**

Tip 1 Read your writing aloud **slowly**. This will help you to check:
- if a word looks right or wrong
- if you have missed a word out or put an extra one in
- if your writing makes sense.

2 **Read these sentences aloud and slowly.**

1 Spot *three* words that look wrong:

We put the worter into the contayner and heeted it up.

2 Spot *one* missing word and *one* extra word.

At full time the score was was 4—2. The winning team around the pitch three times to celebrate.

3 Does this make sense? Spot *three* mistakes.

'Com here at once!' she shout. 'How dare you take money from my purse without asking me fist?'

3 **Read Tip 2.**

> **Tip 2** Put a ruler under each line of your writing. Read each word like a robot. As you read, ask yourself: 'Does it look right?'

4 **Put a ruler under this sentence and spot *three* mistakes.**

> *Viking kings wer brayve warriors who led their men in batle.*

5 **Read Tip 3.**

> **Tip 3** Be smart! Learn the most useful words first!

6 **Read a piece of your own writing.**

> 1 Are there any key words or common words that you often spell wrongly?
> 2 Learn how to spell *five* of them, using a strategy from Unit 19.

7 **Read Tip 4.**

> **Tip 4** Find out what sorts of mistakes you make most.

8 **Copy out this chart.**

What type of mistake?	How many times?	Words to learn
Wrong word endings		
Leaving letters out		
Letters in the wrong order		
Wrong vowels		
Putting too many letters in		

1 Read *three* pieces of your own writing. Fill in the chart as you go:

What type of mistake?	How many times?	Words to learn
Wrong word endings	11	he sing/he sings

2 Try to find a pattern to your mistakes.

9 **Choose your most common type of mistake. Set yourself a target.**

> My target: I will . . .

Heinemann Educational Publishers
Halley Court, Jordan Hill, Oxford OX2 8EJ
Part of Harcourt Limited

Heinemann is the registered trademark of
Harcourt Education Limited

Text © Parts A and B: Jill Baker, Clare Constant, David Kitchen 2002
Text © Part C: Louise Dempsey, Isabel Wright 2002

First published in 2002
06 05 04
10 9 8 7 6 5 4 3

ISBN 0 435 22594 4

Produced by Gecko Ltd, Bicester, Oxon
Original illustrations © Reed Educational & Professional Publishing Ltd 2002
Illustrations by Abigail Conway, Karen Donnelly, Alice Englander, Tony Forbes, Phil Healey, Pantelis Palios,
Kathryn Prewett, Nick Schon, Lisa Smith, Martin Ursell, Sarah Warburton, DTP / Geoff Ward, Jennifer Ward
Cover design by Miller, Craig & Cocking
Printed and bound in Spain by Edelvives

Acknowledgements
**The publishers have made every effort to trace the copyright
holders, but if they have inadvertently overlooked any, they will be
pleased to make the necessary arrangements at the first opportunity.**

Extracts: 'Boo' and 'In The Back Seat' by Kevin Crossley-Holland, from
Short! Published by Oxford University Press. Copyright © Kevin
Crossley-Holland 1998. Reproduced by permission of the author c/o
Rogers Coleridge & White Limited, 20 Powis Mews, London W11 1JN;
from *Truth Or Dare* by Celia Rees, published by Macmillan. Reprinted
with permission of Macmillan; from *Bad Girls* by Jacqueline Wilson,
published by Doubleday/Corgi. Used by permission of Transworld
Publishers, a division of The Random House Group Limited; from
Blabbermouth by Morris Gleitzman, published by Macmillan. Copyright
© 1992 Gleitzman McCaul Pty Ltd. Reprinted by permission of
Macmillan Children's Books, London UK and Macmillan Australia; from
Dakota of the White Flats by Philip Ridley (Puffin 1996), Copyright ©
Philip Ridley, 1989. Reprinted by permission of The Penguin Group UK;
from *Rude Health* by Linda Aronson, published by Macmillan, Copyright
© Linda Aronson, 1999. Reproduced by permission of Macmillan
Children's Books, London, UK, Linda Aronson, and Macmillan Australia;
from 'There's No Such Thing' by Paul Jennings from *Unbelievable*
published by Penguin Books, Australia, and reprinted with permission of
the publishers; from *Remote Man* by Elizabeth Honey published by Allen
& Unwin, Australia in 2000. Reprinted by permission of Allen & Unwin
Book Publishers, Australia. www.allen-unwin.com.au; from *Dangerous
Reality* by Malorie Blackman, published by Doubleday/Corgi. Used by
permission of Transworld Publishers, a division of The Random House
Group Limited; from 'End of the Road' from *Family Frictions* by Kara

May. Copyright © Kara May. Reprinted with the kind permission of the
author; 'The Thingy' by Lindsay MacRae, from *How To Avoid Kissing
Your Parents in Public* published by Puffin, 2000. Copyright © Lindsay
MacRae, 2000. Reprinted with the kind permission of the author; 'It
Was....' by Pip Corbett, from *Rice, Pie & Moses* published by Macmillan.
Reprinted with the kind permission of the author; from *Face* by Benjamin
Zephaniah, published by Bloomsbury. Copyright © Benjamin
Zephaniah, 1999. Reprinted with permission of Bloomsbury; from
Minders by Diana Hendry, published by Walker Books. Copyright ©
1998 Diana Hendry. Reproduced by permission of Walker Books
Limited, London; from *Kensuke's Kingdom* by Michael Morpurgo,
published by Egmont Children's Books. Reprinted by permission of
David Higham Associates Limited; Front Cover from MIZZ magazine,
no. 436, January 23rd – February 5th, 2002. © MIZZ/IPC Syndications.
Reprinted with the kind permission of IPC Syndications; Cover from
DISNEY BIG TIME magazine. Reprinted with permission of Disney Big
Time; Brian Blessed quote, reprinted with the kind permission of Scope;
Extract and logo re Club 18–30. Reprinted with the kind permission of
Club 18–30; from Pontin's 2002 First Edition Brochure. Reprinted with
the kind permission of Pontin's Limited.

**The publishers would like to thank the following for permission to
reproduce photographs on the pages noted.**
Cover: Corbis Stockmarket (keyboard); Image State (traffic lights; open
book); Inside: Imagebank (wide-screen TV, p.45; presenter, p.151;
skateboarder, p.144); Humphrey Gudgeon (rural window, p.64); Corbis
(yacht, p.73; spider, p.104; theme park ride, p.160; sunbathers, p.153;
ravers, p.153); Rex Features (Roald Dahl, p.100; Brian Blessed, p.151);
Empics (football boy, p.144); Photodisk (elderly woman, p.151)

Tel: 01865 888058 www.heinemann.co.uk